BECOMING WHEALTHY

WEALTH AND HEALTH RISING IN SYNC

Mark DiGiovanni

Copyright 2012 Mark DiGiovanni
All rights reserved

BECOMING WHEALTHY

*To Beth,
who always knows where
to stick the commas.*

TABLE OF CONTENTS

INTRODUCTION

Becoming YOU

Becoming INSPIRED & MOTIVATED

Becoming CONNECTED

Becoming UNSTOPPABLE

Becoming EFFICIENT

Becoming SMARTER & WISER

Becoming PHYSICALLY STRONGER

Becoming FISCALLY STRONGER

Becoming WHEALTHY

REFERENCES

BECOMING WHEALTHY

INTRODUCTION

I'm frustrated.

I'm not frustrated with myself or my circumstances. Frankly, I don't deserve half of my good fortune. I'm frustrated over the mass of humanity that hasn't become what they are capable of becoming.

You might think that my motivation to write this book was to help you and millions of others become healthier and wealthier, thereby securing your eternal gratitude and some semblance of immortality. That second part would be nice, but it's the first part that's important. I don't believe there is a person on this planet who wouldn't want to be healthier and wealthier, which means the potential market for this book is about seven billion people. I'd be ecstatic if one percent of one percent of them read this book and derived some benefit from it. My frustration involves those in the 99.99% who *really* need help in this area, but for a multitude of reasons will never get that help.

I'm frustrated that few of us have ever taken a personality evaluation to help us understand the raw material we have within us. Even fewer of us have ever examined our character strengths, which is a prerequisite to developing those strengths.

I'm frustrated that we have to dig through such a trash heap in our culture today to find any true sources of inspiration. Once we do find inspiration, we seem at a loss how to use it properly or how to motivate ourselves when the going gets tough.

I'm frustrated that, in our zeal for autonomy and individuality, we undervalue relationships. We also erroneously think that having several hundred Facebook friends is somehow a substitute for close friends and deep commitments.

I'm frustrated that we seem to know nothing about setting goals, which is the first step in accomplishing anything. For too many of us, the last time we had a set of formal goals with a plan to achieve them was when we were playing sports in high school.

I'm frustrated that we are so adept at acquiring bad habits and so poor at acquiring good ones. Our habits are our character and our character is our destiny. We should focus on learning how to create habits that will be our ally, not our enemy.

I'm frustrated that we have so many choices in so many areas, yet we are untrained and unskilled in how to make good choices. Knowing how to choose is a necessary prerequisite if freedom of choice is going to work for you and not against you.

I'm frustrated that emotions cause us to make so many mistakes in life. Two emotions alone, greed and fear, destroy more fortunes than all the robber barons and Wall Street charlatans combined ever could.

I'm frustrated by what can only be considered a lack of self-control in so many areas by so many people, as evidenced by:

- Two-thirds of Americans are overweight; half of those are now classified as obese.
- One in five Americans still smokes.
- The average monthly car payment exceeds the average monthly contribution to a retirement fund.
- People buying more house than their incomes can support.
- Twenty million Americans use illegal drugs; another thirteen million abuse alcohol.

BECOMING WHEALTHY

- Two babies out of five are born out of wedlock.
- We allow our government to spend 60% more than it collects because no one is willing to accept less or pay more.

These issues frustrate me is because they are at the core of why so many people are less healthy, less wealthy, less successful, and less happy than they could be. A majority of people spend the majority of their lives hoping for some equivalent of alchemy to bring them easy health and instant wealth.

Cher, known more for her sequins than her pearls of wisdom, made a commercial in the 1980's for Bally Fitness where she declared, "If a great body came in a bottle, everybody would have one." She was absolutely correct, yet we still seek such a pill today.

As a financial planner, I can't tell you how many investment schemes I've seen promising extraordinary, "guaranteed" returns, even though the two are mutually exclusive by the laws of economics and human nature.

What is "Whealthy"? Most of us probably don't give too much thought to the interconnectedness of wealth and health. We will notice if a health issue creates a huge expense that decreases our wealth. Beyond that, we tend to view health and wealth through separate lenses. This disconnection is surprising. , Eighty-five percent of us make a connection between health and wealth when we make our most solemn promise. It's typically some variant of the following: "I take you, to be my lawful wedded spouse; to have and to hold, from this day forward; for better, for worse; *for richer, for poorer; in sickness and in health*; to love and to cherish; till death do us part."

BECOMING WHEALTHY

In our wedding vows, we promise to remain together regardless of three varying conditions: better or worse, richer or poorer, sickness or health. These wedding vows date back almost five hundred years, so health and wealth have been affecting the stability of marriages for centuries.

Partners in a marriage generally agree whether they are rich or poor. If one of them is sick, it is usually apparent to both. Determining whether things are better or worse in a marriage depends greatly on whether they are richer or poorer, or in sickness or in health. It can be nice to think that adversity strengthens the bonds of marriage, but that's largely an illusion.

The truth is it's easier to remain married when husband and wife both enjoy health and wealth. Financial issues always rank at or near the top of reasons why couples divorce. Addiction and abuse are in everyone's top ten reasons for divorce. Addiction is the risking of one's own health; abuse is risking the health of one's partner. (Health includes mental, spiritual, and emotional health, as well as physical health; they are all interrelated.)

Becoming whealthy is not about competition. It is not about having more money than someone else. It is not about losing more weight or running more miles than someone else. If you think in terms of trying to do more, be more, or have more than someone else, you will be motivated for all the wrong reasons, and you will find any success surprisingly unsatisfactory.

Becoming whealthy is definitely about improving your health and wealth compared to where you are now, but that means that the only competition is with your present self. An important reason for competing only with your present self is that it's a competition you can control. You have all the tools to improve your health and wealth. You have no ability to control the health and wealth of a perceived competitor. The only person you have to be better than is who you are right now, which is challenge enough.

Becoming whealthy is about maximizing your natural talents. It's about honing new skills to help you reach your full potential. We all have innate talents and strengths which make up the core of who we are. We often don't fully appreciate these gifts because we didn't have to work for them; they just come naturally. Because we often don't fully value our natural talents and strengths, we tend to underutilize them. We achieve less than we are capable of achieving.

Becoming whealthy does require the development of new skills and habits. Much of the book deals with helping you develop skills and habits that will create behaviors that will make improved health and wealth inevitable.

Becoming whealthy is about recognizing behaviors and setting priorities. When you find yourself in a hole, the first thing to do is to stop digging. It is important to recognize behaviors that put us in a hole.

Because the first priority when you're in a hole is to stop digging, the first priority in becoming whealthy is to address those actions that destroy whealth. I refer here to actions that simultaneously destroy both wealth and health. Changing actions that destroy whealth may be the most difficult task, but it also provides the greatest rewards.

The second level of priority includes actions that create whealth, those actions that improve both health and wealth simultaneously. It is relatively easy to get motivated to take such actions because you receive positive reinforcement in two areas. In the first level, where we address actions that destroy whealth, we are stopping a negative action. In the second level, where we address actions that create whealth, we are starting and maintaining a positive action.

The third level of priority includes actions that harm either health or wealth. Even though the most important thing to do when you're in a hole is to stop digging, taking actions that create wealth and health take priority over taking actions that harm either wealth or health.

Taking actions that create whealth produce twice the benefits, compared to actions that merely harm wealth or health. Second, we all need positive reinforcement to keep us motivated. Receiving positive reinforcement from taking actions that create and improve whealth provides the incentive we need to keep working on the third and fourth levels of priority.

The fourth level of priority includes actions that improve health or wealth. These actions, while still important, are less likely to have the return on investment that the other three levels provide. For people with a competitive nature, once you've accomplished everything in the first three levels, actions at this level are what separate the elites from the pack.

There are no universal measurements to determine if someone has become whealthy. Everyone has different standards for what they consider to be either healthy or wealthy. Standards are based on many factors, not the least of which is a comparison with other people. For example, the standard for wealth is very different in the U.S. than in Haiti.

Within a specific population, there isn't likely to be a huge discrepancy in the standards for health, wealth, or whealth. Again, this discrepancy is due to our tendency to set our standards by what we see around us. Going back to the U.S.-Haiti comparison, Haitians might consider the attainment of a regular supply of clean drinking water to be a major upgrade in their health standard. Americans would consider any irregular supply of clean drinking water to be an unacceptable standard altogether. When we get outside our immediate circle, we see how people have different standards and how they vary greatly in what is most important.

One society may rate wealth far more important than health. The United States as a whole would fall into this category. Other countries place a higher value on health than wealth. Most of the Scandinavian countries would fall into this category. Many people look at health and wealth through very different lenses, so that when you combine those two lenses into whealth, the number of different visions and versions is almost immeasurable.

One commonality of health and wealth is that it is often defined more by its absence than its presence. Most of us don't recognize or appreciate our good health until we become ill or injured. Because we define whealth more by its absence than its presence, we are more likely to be aware of when we are not whealthy than when we are.

How can you know if you are sufficiently whealthy, or what standard you should use to determine where you are and where you should aim to be? On the wealth side, one standard that can be applied is, if your income is greater than your expenses, and if your expenses are equal to your desires, then you are wealthy. This standard gives you three variables you can control - income, expenses, and desire. At a minimum, most people would define wealth after retirement as having all the assets necessary to maintain one's independence and dignity during that period.

Maintaining one's independence and dignity is also a good starting point for setting a standard for health. No one wants to be a burden to others. Being dependent on others is a sure way to forfeit one's independence and dignity.

The first standard for health should be the standard that we take care of our physical needs to the fullest extent possible. When we're young and maintaining our health isn't an effort, we must still make an effort to maintain it. One day our health will begin to fail us. The more we can do to forestall that day, the longer we can maintain our independence and dignity.

Becoming whealthy is not easy; it doesn't have to be hard, either. As with any task, there are ways that give you the maximum return for the effort. The purpose of this book is to help you understand what will pay benefits, not only in becoming whealthy, but will enable you to become more successful and happy in life overall.

Becoming YOU

THE MAN (OR WOMAN) YOU ARE by Ted Olsen

*It isn't the man you might have been
Had the chance been yours again,
Nor the prize you wanted but didn't win
That weighs in the measure of men.
No futile "if" or poltroon "because"
Can rowel your stock to par.
The world cares naught for what never was;
It judges by what you are.*

*It isn't the man you hope to be,
If fortune and fate are kind,
That the chill, keen eyes of the world will see
In weighing your will and mind.
The years ahead are a chartless sea,
And tomorrow's a world away.
It isn't the man you'd like to be,
But the man you are today.*

*There's little worth in the phantom praise
Of a time that may never dawn,
And less in a vain regret for days
And deeds long buried and gone.
There's little time on this busy earth
To argue the why and how.
The game is yours if you prove your worth,
And prove it here and now!*

I am an ENFJ. Sometimes I'm an ENTJ.

Carl Jung (1875-1961) was an eminent Swiss psychiatrist and the founder of analytical psychology. Among other things, Jung gave us the concept of the introvert and the extrovert.

According to Jung's typology, every individual can be classified using these three criteria:

- **Extroversion – Introversion**
- **Sensing – Intuition**
- **Thinking – Feeling**

Isabel Briggs-Myers (1897-1980), a noted American psychiatrist, added a fourth criterion:

- **Judging – Perceiving**

Isabel, along with her mother, Katharine Briggs, developed the Myers-Briggs Type Indicator (MBTI). The MBTI is not a test, in that tests have right and wrong answers. The MBTI is a personality inventory in which there are no right or wrong answers. It is designed to measure how people perceive the world and make decisions.

The four criteria are defined as follows:

- "The first criterion, **Extroversion - Introversion** defines the source and direction of energy expression for a person. The extrovert has a source and direction of energy expression mainly in the external world while the introvert has a source of energy mainly in the internal world.
- The second criterion, **Sensing - iNtuition** defines the method of information perception by a person. Sensing means that a person believes mainly information he or she receives directly from the external world. Intuition means that a person believes mainly information he/she receives from the internal or imaginative world.

- The third criterion, **Thinking** - **Feeling** defines how the person processes information. Thinking means that a person makes a decision mainly through logic. Feeling means that, as a rule, he/she makes a decision based on emotion.
- The fourth criterion, **Judging** - **Perceiving** defines how a person implements the information he/she has processed. Judging means that a person organizes all his/her life events and acts strictly according to his/her plans. Perceiving means that he/she is inclined to improvise and seek alternatives."

Different combinations of these criteria determine a personality type. There are sixteen types. Every type has a name, based on the combination of criteria. The sixteen types are listed below, with the percentage of the U.S. population that falls into each type:

ISTJ-11.6%	ISFJ-13.8%	INFJ-1.5%	INTJ-2.1%
ISTP-5.4%	ISFP-8.8%	INFP-4.3%	INTP-3.3%
ESTP-4.3%	ESFP-8.5%	ENFP-8.1%	ENTP-3.2%
ESTJ-8.7%	ESFJ-12.3%	ENFJ-2.4%	ENTJ-1.8%

Here is more detailed information about these eight different personality traits and the people who possess them:

EXTROVERTS:
- Are energized by being with other people;
- Like being the center of attention;
- Act, then think;
- Tend to think out loud;
- Are easier to read and know, share personal information freely;

- Talk more than listen;
- Communicate with enthusiasm;
- Respond quickly, enjoy a fast pace;
- Prefer breadth to depth.

INTROVERTS:
- Are energized by spending time alone;
- Avoid being the center of attention;
- Think, then act;
- Think things through inside their head;
- Are more private, prefer to share personal information with a select few;
- Listen more than talk;
- Keep their enthusiasm to themselves;
- Respond after taking the time to think things through, enjoy a slower pace;
- Prefer depth to breadth.

SENSORS:
- Trust what is certain and concrete;
- Like new ideas only if they have practical application;
- Value realism and common sense;
- Like to use and hone established skills;
- Tend to be specific and literal, give detailed descriptions;
- Present information in a step-by-step manner;
- Are oriented to the present.

INTUITIVES:
- Trust inspiration and inference;
- Like new ideas and concepts for their own sake;
- Value imagination and innovation;
- Like to learn new skills, get bored easily after mastering skills;

- Tend to be general and figurative, use metaphors and analogies;
- Present information through leaps, in a roundabout manner;
- Are oriented toward the future.

THINKERS:
- Step back and apply impersonal analysis to problems;
- Value logic, justice, and fairness; one standard for all;
- Naturally see flaws and tend to be critical;
- May be seen as heartless, insensitive, and uncaring;
- Consider it more important to be truthful than tactful.

FEELERS:
- Step forward, consider the effect of actions on others;
- Value empathy and harmony;
- Naturally like to please others, show appreciation easily;
- May be seen as overemotional, illogical, and weak;
- Consider it important to be tactful as well as truthful.

JUDGERS:
- Are happiest after decisions have been made;
- Have a work ethic - work first, play later;
- Set goals and work toward achieving them on time;
- Prefer knowing what they are getting into;
- Emphasize completion of the task;
- Derive satisfaction from finishing projects;
- See time as a finite resource and take deadlines seriously.

PERCEIVERS:
- Are happiest leaving their options open;
- Have a play ethic - play now, work later;

- Change goals as new information becomes available;
- Like adapting to new situations;
- Emphasize how a task is completed;
- Derive satisfaction from starting projects;
- See time as a renewable resource.

The following synopsis of each of the sixteen personality types is excerpted from Introduction to Type by Isabel Briggs Myers, published by CPP. Inc.:

ISTJ
Quiet, serious, earn success by thoroughness and dependability. Practical, matter-of-fact, realistic, and responsible. Decide logically what should be done and work toward it steadily, regardless of distractions. Take pleasure in making everything orderly and organized – their work, their home, their life. Value traditions and loyalty.

ISFJ
Quiet, friendly, responsible, and conscientious. Committed and steady in meeting their obligations. Thorough, painstaking, and accurate. Loyal, considerate, notice and remember specifics about people who are important to them, concerned with how others feel. Strive to create an orderly and harmonious environment at work and at home.

INFJ
Seek meaning and connection in ideas, relationships, and material possessions. Want to understand what motivates people and are insightful about others. Conscientious and committed to their firm values. Develop a clear

vision about how best to serve the common good. Organized and decisive in implementing their vision.

INTJ
Have original minds and great drive for implementing their ideas and achieving their goals. Quickly see patterns in external events and develop long-range explanatory perspectives. When committed, organize a job and carry it through. Skeptical and independent, have high standards of competence and performance – for themselves and others.

ISTP
Tolerant and flexible, quiet observers until a problem appears, then act quickly to find workable solutions. Analyze what makes things work and readily get through large amounts of data to isolate the core of practical problems. Interested in cause and effect, organize facts using logical principles, value efficiency.

ISFP
Quiet, friendly, sensitive, and kind. Enjoy the present moment, what's going on around them. Like to have their own space and to work within their own time frame. Loyal and committed to their values and to people who are important to them. Dislike disagreements and conflicts, do not force their opinions or values on others.

INFP
Idealistic, loyal to their values and to people who are important to them. Want an external life that is congruent with their values. Curious, quick to see possibilities, can be catalysts for implementing ideas.

Seek to understand people and to help them fulfill their potential. Adaptable, flexible, and accepting unless a value is threatened.

INTP
Seek to develop logical explanations for everything that interests them. Theoretical and abstract, interested more in ideas than in social interaction. Quiet, contained, flexible, and adaptable. Have unusual ability to focus in depth to solve problems in their area of interest. Skeptical, sometimes critical, always analytical.

ESTP
Flexible and tolerant, they take a pragmatic approach focused on immediate results. Theories and conceptual explanations bore them – they want to act energetically to solve the problem. Focus on the here-and-now, spontaneous, enjoy each moment that they can be active with others. Enjoy material comforts and style. Learn best through doing.

ESFP
Outgoing, friendly, and accepting. Exuberant lovers of life, people, and material comforts. Enjoy working with others to make things happen. Bring common sense and a realistic approach to their work, and make work fun. Flexible and spontaneous, adapt readily to new people and environments. Learn best by trying a new skill with other people.

ENFP
Warmly enthusiastic and imaginative. See life as full of possibilities. Make connections between events and information very quickly, and confidently proceed based

on the patterns they see. Want a lot of affirmation from others, and readily give appreciation and support. Spontaneous and flexible, often rely on their ability to improvise and their verbal fluency.

ENTP
Quick, ingenious, stimulating, alert, and outspoken. Resourceful in solving new and challenging problems. Adept at generating conceptual possibilities and then analyzing them strategically. Good at reading other people. Bored by routine, will seldom do the same thing the same way, apt to turn to one new interest after another.

ESTJ
Practical, realistic, matter-of-fact. Decisive, quickly move to implement decisions. Organize projects and people to get things done, focus on getting results in the most efficient way possible. Take care of routine details. Have a clear set of logical standards, systematically follow them and want others to also. Forceful in implementing their plans.

ESFJ
Warmhearted, conscientious, and cooperative. Want harmony in their environment, work with determination to establish it. Like to work with others to complete tasks accurately and on time. Loyal, follow through even in small matters. Notice what others need in their day-by-day lives and try to provide it. Want to be appreciated for who they are and for what they contribute.

ENFJ
Warm, empathetic, responsive, and responsible. Highly

attuned to the emotions, needs, and motivations of others. Find potential in everyone, want to help others fulfill their potential. May act as catalysts for individual and group growth. Loyal, responsive to praise and criticism. Sociable, facilitate others in a group, and provide inspiring leadership.

ENTJ
Frank, decisive, assume leadership readily. Quickly see illogical and inefficient procedures and policies, develop and implement comprehensive systems to solve organizational problems. Enjoy long-term planning and goal setting. Usually well informed, well read, enjoy expanding their knowledge and passing it on to others. Forceful in presenting their ideas.

Because everyone ends up in one of only sixteen types, people within a type can still vary widely in terms of their overall personalities. We can, however, look at the eight personality traits to get an indication of how someone who possesses those traits is likely to act and react in matters affecting their health and wealth.

When you think of extroverts and money, you may picture someone on CNBC talking about the latest can't-miss investment strategy. That person is almost certainly an extrovert, though hardly representative of extroverts in general.

Extroverts tend to act before thinking, which can lead to some regrettable decisions regarding their health and wealth. Their bias for action also puts them in the lead in many new ventures. Extroverts are more likely to be in on the ground floor of some game-changing new products and services. Extroverts are like the baseball player who leads the league in home runs *and* strikeouts.

Extroverts enjoy a fast pace and are quick responders. Extroverts prefer breadth to depth and are likely to have their thumbs in many pies and many irons in the fire. Their investment portfolio is likely to have a large number of stocks and more exotic investments. Extroverts are likely to buy investments on the high-risk-high-return end of the spectrum.

Because they seek out social relationships more than introverts, extroverts are more likely to reap the benefits of those relationships, such as a greater sense of well-being and lower levels of stress. A study in 2009 by researchers at the University of Rochester suggests personality, not just factors like race or gender, affects our ability to withstand stress-related, inflammatory diseases. The study found that extroverts, and in particular those with high "dispositional activity" or engagement in life, have dramatically lower levels of the inflammatory chemical interleukin 6 (IL-6).

Extroverts may also be more inclined to take care of their physical appearance because of the value they place on the acceptance and approval of others. The desire to look good can help maintain good health, as the extrovert may be less inclined to become obese or to abuse drugs and alcohol.

When you think of introverts and money, you may picture an economics professor with a bow tie and sweater vest, working on a new method to calculate standard deviation. Such an introvert would be more interested in developing a new economic theory than in discussing it on CNN.

Introverts think first and then act. They are slow and deliberate. It is more important for them to get it right than to get it right now. Introverts listen more than they talk. They will gather as much information as possible in order to make the most informed decision possible. This trait can cause them to develop information overload, which can lead to decision paralysis.

Introverts prefer depth to breadth. To that end, they are unlikely to invest in areas that are unfamiliar or opaque, such as derivatives or other investments whose true value is hard to ascertain. They are likely to hold fewer stocks in their portfolio than extroverts, but they will have more in-depth knowledge of the companies they own.

Introverts won't hit a lot of home runs; they won't strike out much, either. They will not get rich overnight; they may get rich over time. Introverts do not necessarily favor security over opportunity, nor do extroverts necessarily favor the opposite.

Research shows that the brains of introverts are more active than the brains of extroverts. Introverts prefer to exercise their minds while extroverts prefer to exercise their jaws. There is a bias in professional and lay circles that extroverts are happier than introverts. Studies have led to this conclusion, though the testing methods may favor the way extroverts choose to express happiness.

The worst aspect of introversion from a health standpoint is that the introvert may feel pressure to become an extrovert. There is nothing wrong with preferring to read a book than to go to a party. Introverts try to become extroverts far more than extroverts try to become introverts. This disparity may explain in part the lower stress levels of extroverts; they're not trying to be something they aren't.

Introverts tend to favor quality over quantity and specialization over generalization, as compared to extroverts. Introverts are more likely to practice moderation in their habits, which can serve them well in the areas of health. Introverts prefer to do a few things and to do them well, which can lead to a greater sense of accomplishment. Introverts are less likely to need the approval of others to boost their self-esteem.

Sensors trust what is certain and concrete, though they may eventually find little to trust in a world filled with uncertainty. During the long bull market of the 1980's and 1990's, sensors trusted that the stock market would continue in an upward trajectory indefinitely. When the first decade of the 21st century saw two of the worst bear markets since the Great Depression, the trust of the sensors was severely shaken. Once sensors lose trust in something, it may never return. Many sensors may never return to the stock market after the experiences of recent years.

Sensors are not likely to be on the vanguard of something new, due to their preference for using established skills and ideas that have an immediate practical application. They will be more conservative in most life choices, including how they save, spend, and invest their money. Sensors are specific and literal, which means you are not likely to convince them of something by appealing to their imagination.

Sensors are oriented to the present, which is not to say that they don't plan for the future. Their vision of the future is grounded in the present, so they plan for the future based on what they are certain of in the present. One drawback to this strategy is that the constant change of modern life means that what is certain today may not be at all certain in the future. During stable times, sensors fare quite well. Rapid change requires adaptability, with which sensors often need help.

Because sensors are more oriented to the present, it can be difficult to get them to imagine themselves as old when they are younger. A forty-year-old sensor may have difficulty imagining how the health habits of today will affect his/her health in three decades. Aging well is a process of adaptation, which is not a strong suit of the sensor.

Intuitives make up the great majority of entrepreneurs. When I say entrepreneur, I mean someone who loves to take an idea and make it a reality. True entrepreneurs are more missionary than mercenary, and being intuitive is a great asset in that line of work.

Intuitives like new ideas for their own sake, so they may find themselves investing in concepts that turn out to have no economic benefit. Because they are open to new ideas and concepts, they are also more likely to see the potential in an idea before everyone else does, causing them to be the leaders in new fields. Imagination and innovation are highly valued, so the best and brightest are drawn to work with intuitives.

Intuitives are oriented to the future, which is why so many of their ventures pay off. They see now what becomes obvious to the rest of us only much later. The downside to such a future orientation is a lack of attention to the present. More often than not, the Intuitive is derailed not by a bad idea, but by inattention to present realities, which can upset the best-laid plans.

Although intuitives are oriented to the future, that doesn't mean they are taking good care of themselves in the present. Good health today is the product of yesterday's habits, and good health tomorrow is the product of today's habits. The focus on the future often means the drudgery of the present is avoided, and good health does require a certain measure of drudgery in the present.

Thinkers are very left-brain people. Their minds are like high-powered computers. There are some paradoxes with Thinkers. They value justice and fairness, but are viewed as heartless and insensitive. They view themselves as holding on to principles; others view them as rigid and unfeeling.

Thinkers are capable of stepping back and applying impersonal analysis to problems. This trait makes them very good at getting to the unvarnished truth. When something is going wrong in a business, Thinkers are the ones who will roll up their sleeves and figure out what needs to be done. Because they value truth more than tact, when they report their findings to management, they may do so in a way that actually gets in the way of needed reform.

Because Thinkers are more accurately *critical* thinkers, they are good at finding flaws. This perspective also tends to make Thinkers more pessimistic than the general population; they will see the glass as half-empty, as well as dirty and chipped. A pessimistic outlook combined with a frustration over the imperfections of life can inhibit Thinkers from taking long-term risks for long-term rewards. Thinkers may eschew owning stocks, even for long-term investment goals because of the fear that the human faults that affect the system, such as securities fraud, will cause their investments to not perform the way cold analysis indicates they should. Thinkers are good at putting the brakes on activities that are going too fast. Brakes alone don't go anywhere, though. Thinkers need relationships with those who move forward to avoid stagnation.

BECOMING WHEALTHY

Thinkers will take care of their health only if it is logical to do so. They will be motivated by statistics on heart disease, not by a commercial for an energy drink. The natural pessimism of thinkers can not only be a liability to good health in the present (pessimism is far more stressful than optimism), such pessimism can also make it harder to imagine a future that is worth making any sacrifices for in the present.

Feelers are team players. They value empathy and harmony and are always considerate of the feelings of others. They will not gain at the expense of others and may be more inclined to be taken advantage of by others. In a competitive environment, Feelers will have a problem, and they will not choose a tournament-style conflict if there are alternatives.

While Feelers may not be the best types to fill the role of traders on the floor of the New York Stock Exchange, they may be the best types to fill the role of consultative financial advisors in the 21st century. Because they understand the human aspect in any situation better than most, they are better equipped to motivate people to action. Thinkers may be great at knowing which direction people should go, but it usually takes Feelers to actually get the people moving in that direction.

Feelers' biggest problem from a health standpoint is probably their inclination to put others first all the time. They are more likely to ignore their own needs while taking care of others' wants. As a result, they may not take the time to eat right, exercise, or get enough sleep.

Feelers are cooperative, not competitive. Because of this nature, Feelers may not fare as well in the short term. However, in the long term, Feelers will fare better than most others because the more long-term the goals are, the more cooperation, rather than competition, is needed to achieve them. Feelers are not combative, and they might lose many battles. They are more likely to end up winning a war, though.

Judgers are not likely to end up being supported by their children in their old age. They are very good at setting goals and working toward achieving them by the deadline. Judgers are motivated by the satisfaction they get from completing a project. Nothing makes them happier than setting a goal of being financially independent by a certain date and actually achieving that independence.

Judgers believe in business before pleasure. They will make sure that all financial obligations (including obligations to themselves) are met before they spend money on items like vacations or luxury cars. They also are likely to succeed in starting their own businesses because they are more likely to make the sacrifices necessary in the early years to enable a business to succeed in the long run.

Judgers are deadline-conscious, so they value time as a finite, exhaustible resource. This trait is mostly useful because it encourages careful use of time. Judgers can also put unnecessary pressure on themselves to complete a task on time, which can sometimes result in compromises in quality, or even major errors in judgment. Strict adherence to deadlines can confine Judgers when flexibility may be the more valuable trait.

Judgers are more likely to do the drudgery required to maintain their health. They will get up an hour early to go for a run before work. They will get regular checkups and make sure their cholesterol is always in the acceptable range. They are also more likely to see activities like exercise only as the means to an end, not the end in itself.

Perceivers are recognized for their flexibility and adaptability, but they can sometimes resemble a boat with a sail and no rudder. The desire to keep their options open can cause them to avoid setting goals.

Perceivers enjoy the mechanics of completing a task more than the accomplishment of the task itself. They are good at developing the tactics necessary to implement the strategy that was created by others. They can adapt as new information becomes available, though they are not likely to be the ones generating that new information.

Perceivers see time as a renewable resource, so they are prone to find themselves out of time. For them, it's pleasure before business, which is not a good plan for becoming whealthy. Perceivers may be more inclined to work to a much older age, in part because they still see themselves as young and vital, but also because they may have procrastinated in taking concrete steps to enable them to afford to retire. In the Aesop's fable, the ants would have been Judgers; the grasshopper, a Perceiver.

Perceivers may not suffer from stress, but they may suffer long-term health problems if they procrastinated on taking care of themselves. Because they are reactive, not proactive, Perceivers are less likely to deal with a health problem until they have no option but to deal with it, which by then might be too late.

When it comes to becoming whealthy, there is no magic personality type. When reading the characteristics of the eight different personality traits, it can be tempting to think that a certain combination is the magic formula for health and wealth. Because every human is unique, no one possesses these personality traits in the exact same combination as anyone else. We are like snowflakes in that respect; the ingredients may be simple, but the product is endlessly varied.

There is another use for these personality evaluations that may be even more important than determining if you need help in monitoring your health or managing your finances. The MBTI can be very helpful in assessing your strengths and weaknesses to help you align your career path with your personality.

One reason why so many people have dismal finances, dismal health, and a dismal future is because they are doing work that is not well suited to them. If you are in a job that doesn't mesh with your personality, you aren't going to be very good at it. If you aren't very good at your job, you aren't likely to be happy or healthy, and you aren't likely to be well paid for it, either.

Personality evaluations can help you find a career that better suits your personality and your strengths, which should enable you to do a better job and make more money. More importantly, getting into a career that fits your personality will greatly increase your chances for happiness on the job, as well as success on the job.

We are all familiar with the phrase "Be yourself." It's a vague instruction, subject to endless interpretation. It's also frequently invoked to encourage someone to stop imitating someone else. It often gets interpreted as tacit approval for to do whatever you please, with the defense that your actions were merely the expression of you being yourself.

I am all in favor of people being true to themselves. However, I would not give carte blanche to any behavior by encouraging someone to "Be yourself." I would tighten the reins and raise the bar by extolling them not to "Be yourself," but instead to "Be your *best* self."

We all have a personality, even if we never spent a moment developing it. If your personality is the raw material, then your character is the finished product. Your personality is you - your character is You. Knowing your personality type enables you to "Be Yourself." Developing your character enables you to "Be Your Best Self."

Martin Seligman and Chris Peterson are pioneers in the area of positive psychology. For decades, psychology has been focused to the point of obsession on the negative aspects of human personality. Seligman and Peterson have been working to shift that focus to understanding the upper reaches of human health, talent, and possibility.

As their first step in this process, Seligman and Peterson scoured every list of virtues they could find, from religious teachings to the Boy Scout Oath. They discovered that six broad virtues appeared on nearly every list: wisdom, courage, humanity, justice, temperance, and transcendence (the ability to forge connections to something beyond the self). The value of this list of six virtues is as an organizing framework for more specific *strengths of character*. There are several paths to each virtue, and different cultures vary in the degree to which they value each path. The value of the classifications is as a guide to specific means of growth toward widely valued ends, without insisting that any one way is mandatory or even best.

Seligman and Peterson suggest there are twenty-four principle character strengths which lead to one of the six higher-level virtues. You can diagnose your strengths and take several other evaluations at the Authentic Happiness Testing Center at the site developed by Seligman, www.authentichappiness.org. Here are the virtues and their attendant strengths:

- **WISDOM**: curiosity, love of learning, judgment, ingenuity, emotional intelligence, perspective
- **COURAGE**: valor, perseverance, integrity
- **HUMANITY**: kindness, loving
- **JUSTICE**: citizenship, fairness, leadership
- **TEMPERANCE**: self-control, prudence, humility
- **TRANSCENDENCE**: appreciation of beauty and excellence, gratitude, hope, spirituality, forgiveness, humor, zest

Everyone will have a different opinion on the relative value of each of these strengths, and there is no scale that determines the relative value of each. It is perfectly natural that we will give higher value to those strengths which we possess to a higher degree.

Sociology professor William A. Sadler, author of The *Third Age*, has developed six paradoxical principles as steps for growth as we age. While his focus has been on helping people find renewal in their later years, these principles are applicable for every adult at any age.

Principle One: Balancing Mindful Reflection & Risk-Taking - As we age, we operate more and more as if by remote control. Our mindset becomes more narrow, inflexible, repetitive, and automatic. This state of mindlessness, the opposite of mindfulness, interferes with healthy adaptation. Mindlessness, which is often demonstrated through rigid stereotypical thinking, is detrimental to learning and shortchanges our potential. Mindlessness manifests itself in status quo bias, which is the enemy of change, yet change is the essential ingredient to progress. In order to become anything more than you are now, you must first take some time, stop doing what you've been doing, and give yourself the opportunity to reflect on how you want your life to be different, to reflect on what and who you wish to become.

Principle Two: Developing Realistic Optimism - Optimism tends to be a depleting resource as we age, and the economic problems of recent times have taken a toll on everyone's supply of optimism. Pessimism and its mutant offspring, cynicism, keep us from seeing the value in persistence and staying the course when times get hard. Optimism does not deny the prospect of failure. The difference between optimism and pessimism is in how we treat our failures. Optimism acknowledges the prospect of failure and will convert it into a learning experience. Pessimism prevents us from even attempting a task because we see failure as the likely outcome.

Principle Three: Creating a Positive Identity - Continuous self-redefinition is increasingly recognized as an essential element of healthy adult development. One of the paradoxes of life is that success in creating our current life holds us back from creating an even better one. We like to believe that if it ain't broke, don't fix it, but, as Voltaire explained, good is the enemy of great. Few people make the effort to change their lives until it is undeniably broken. Just because your life doesn't appear to be broken doesn't mean there aren't many ways in which it could be better. The people who take their lives from good to great are those who are willing to make changes and exert effort to grow, even when the status quo is comfortable.

Principle Four: Balancing Work and Play - Most of the jobs that people aspire to have today are also the types of jobs that can follow you anywhere because there is some electronic device that makes the job portable. As a result, fewer people have the ability to leave their work completely when they are not on the job. Work has a natural tendency to encroach into other areas, whereas play is rarely allowed to enter the domain of work. It can be an exhausting and often futile battle to limit work's encroachment, so an alternative would be to find work that doesn't feel like work. Mark Twain gave us these definitions - work is what you have to do; play is what you want to do. Finding work that feels like play (at least most of the time) largely eliminates the need to find a balance that won't be kept or to set a border that won't be respected.

Principle Five: Balancing Personal Freedom and Intimacy - Nowhere are the paradoxes of life more evident than in our relationships. The desire to be whoever we want and do whatever we want runs into a major obstacle if we also want to have serious and long-lasting relationships with other people. Marriage is the most obvious example of this paradox. In order to have the kind of relationship with your spouse that will create a successful marriage, that kind of relationship must also be unique with your spouse. If we choose total personal freedom, we may enjoy who we are and what we do, but we may also find ourselves alone and lonely.

Principle Six: Building a More Caring Life - This principle addresses those for whom we care and to what we give care. Before we can determine *who* and *what* we want to give care, we have to determine *why* we want to give that care. One of the signs of personal growth is the evolution to whom and what we give care. When we are young and immature, our care is internally directed. We care about ourselves and about pleasure in the present. Over time, as we take our roles in the world and accept responsibilities, we begin to care more for others, especially those who will follow us. We also begin to care more about non-material things and about our impact on the world after we are gone.

Harry Moody, Ph.D. is another leading researcher in the field of aging. In charting the spiritual passages that shape our lives, he has developed what he calls The Five Stages of the Soul:

- *Stage One: The Call* - The Call is known by many names - conversion, summons, change of heart. The Call can be like a second wind to someone who may feel that life has become little more than wearisome routine. The Call is like hearing the roar of the ocean from a distance for the first time. As long as you hear it, you know the ocean exists. You then become drawn to reach the ocean to see the source of the roar.
- *Stage Two: The Search* - The Search is our response to the call. For most of us, The Search begins with the quest for guidance. The choices here run the gamut from AA to Zen Buddhism. At the conscious level, The Search is for a spiritual practice that fits us. Once we find a teaching that fits us, we search for the place within us where our spiritual impulse lives and grows. On a deeper level, The Search is for "the secret God behind the gods," as Emerson put it.
- *Stage Three: The Struggle* - Once the euphoria of spiritual awakening fades, the quest itself involves tests, trials, and tribulations. Here we struggle with

disillusionment, regret, depression, impatience, and a sense of futility. The demons faced during The Struggle may take the form of faithless lovers, ungrateful children, chronic disease, and countless others. It is at this stage that our faith, however we define it, is tested. To reach our goal, we must persevere through this time. In this sense, The Struggle *is* the way.

- **Stage Four: The Breakthrough** - The Breakthrough comes at the moment when the spiritual forces collecting inside us can no longer be held in check. When The Breakthrough comes, we realize that achieving The Breakthrough is the reason why we are born and why we struggle. Although inevitably illuminating, there are many levels of Breakthrough experiences, some temporary, some permanent, some small, and some great. The Breakthrough is when we connect to "the Infinite within us."
- **Stage Five: The Return** - The Breakthrough changes a person forever. However, as the Zen proverb tells us: "Before enlightenment, you chop wood and carry water. After enlightenment, you chop wood and carry water." Life goes on as before, including the drudgery. There is still work to be done, including further spiritual progress to be made. However, at this stage we can share our experience with the world, which we do by becoming a humanitarian, someone devoted to the promotion of human welfare.

In addition to recognizing our personality type and developing our character strengths, the process of Becoming You requires two "activities" that many of us find hard to perform - Silence and Service. Silence enables us to receive. Service enables us to give.

Silence is a rare commodity today. Between cell phones, the internet, satellite TV, and countless other 24/7 distractions, it's more difficult than ever to find a time and place to simply *be still*.

Imagine living in America two centuries ago. There was a 90% chance you lived in a rural environment. Though you worked hard, there was time to be still. At the end of the day, you might sit outside and look at the stars for an hour or two. (When was the last time you did that, assuming you can even see the stars where you live?) The only communication with others was in person or through print, and since the majority of the population was illiterate, the written word was less pervasive. You may not have always enjoyed that level of silence back then, but at least there was the opportunity for it.

If someone from that era were tossed into the present, he/she would be overcome by the constant bombardment of noise from every quarter. If the sheer volume of the noise did not induce some kind of breakdown in this transplant, the tone of the noise might just do it. Even the noise that is not overtly hostile has an insistence to it, such as advertising that demands to be heard.

We've all experienced the frustration of trying to come up with a new idea or a solution to a problem and working our brains to the white meat to find an answer, to no avail. We finally step away from the problem, and in a totally unrelated moment, when we aren't thinking about anything, least of all that elusive answer, it comes to us in a flash. These are often called *Eureka Moments*, which is defined as a moment of sudden, *unexpected* discovery.

BECOMING WHEALTHY

There are literally hundreds of answers to questions we have on our minds and in our souls that are out there, waiting for us to hear them. We can't hear them, though, because there must first be silence for them to enter. We are so programmed to be proactive about everything that we feel the need to find every answer we seek. It is much healthier, more productive, and more efficient to set aside time on a regular basis to be silent and give the answers we seek the opportunity to *find us*. Becoming You requires both activity and passivity. Finding the proper balance of the two is also part of the process of Becoming You.

Serving our fellow human beings is a key ingredient to being human ourselves. Without an element of service in your life, there will always be a missing piece. You might become You, but it is unlikely that you will become the You that you most desire to become. We all want to be valued by the world. We are valued by the world only to the extent that we add value to the rest of the world, which is the essence of service above self.

Within this realm of service, there is a caveat. Humans are results-oriented by nature, and Americans have raised it to an art form. Everyone knows what *the bottom line* means, even if they never took an accounting class and have no idea what debits or credits are. We are focused on *outcomes*, but service is, or should be, focused on *inputs*.

Much of our frustration and unhappiness in life stem from our attempts to create certain outcomes. This frustration is the result of thinking we have the ability to control outcomes. We don't. All we can control are inputs. If we create the right inputs, we create the possibility that we will get the desired outcome, although it is never guaranteed. An attempt to control outcomes, especially when the proper inputs have been lacking, is what we call cheating.

In performing service for others, we can get frustrated when they don't reciprocate with the outcomes we desire. We help those in need, but get frustrated when they don't seem to want to help themselves to the extent we think they should. We want our service to be appreciated. More important, we want our service to have significance, and when the outcomes don't match our inputs, we feel that our work has no significance and we become frustrated and quit.

Becoming You, at least to become your best You, requires an element of service. As you undertake service, whatever form that service may take, remember that the important part is the service itself, not the results.

Jacob Needleman, philosophy professor and author of *Money and the Meaning of Life,* says that man can be defined as a being constructed to receive a gift of unfathomable immensity and is, at the same time, obliged to pay for that gift with unfathomable commitment and service. This relationship is another of life's paradoxes. We must pay a steep price for something that is freely given. In this context, the aim of personal gain is clear - we gain in order to give; we are served so that we may serve.

You may be wondering why, in a book whose purpose is to help you become whealthy, your first chapter is about topics like personality and character, silence and service. These topics would seem to offer few answers on how to lower your cholesterol or raise your income.

Before you can know *what to do*, you must first understand *who you are*, and you must also understand who you can become. *Who* you can become determines *what* you can become.

You are not your possessions, your balance sheet, or even the reflection you see in the mirror. You are not the bottom line of your health or your wealth. You are not defined by your whealth because whealth is an outcome, not an input. You are the product of your inputs, your personality, and the character you are developing even now. You are not the product of outcomes, even an outcome as desirable as whealth.

BECOMING WHEALTHY

Becoming INSPIRED & MOTIVATED

THE RACE by Dee Groberg

Quit, give up, you're beaten, they shout and beg and plead.
There's just too much against you now. This time you can't succeed.
And as I start to hang my head in front of failure's face,
My downward fall is broken by the memory of a race.
And hope refills my weakened will as I recall that scene.
For just the thought of that short race rejuvenates my being.

A children's race - young boys, young men - how I remember well.
Excitement, sure - but also fear - it wasn't hard to tell.
They all lined up so full of hope, each thought to win that race,
Or tie for first, or if not that, at least take second place.
And fathers watched from off the side, each cheering for his son.
And each boy hoped to show his dad that he would be the one.

The whistle blew, and off they went, young hearts and hopes of fire.
To win, to be the hero there was each young boy's desire.
And one boy in particular, whose dad was in the crowd,
Was running near the lead and thought, "My dad will be so proud!"
But as he sped on down the field across the shallow dip,
The little boy who thought to win lost his step, and slipped.

Trying hard to catch himself, his hands flew out to brace.

BECOMING WHEALTHY

Amid the gasping of the crowd he fell flat on his face.
So, down he fell and with him hope; he couldn't win it now.
Embarrassed, sad, he only wished to disappear somehow.
But, as he fell, his dad stood up, and showed his anxious face,
Which, to the boy, so clearly said, "Get up - and win the race!"

He quickly rose - no damage done - behind a bit, that's all.
He ran with all his heart and might to make up for his fall.
So anxious to restore himself, to catch up, and to win,
His mind went faster than his legs; he slipped and fell again.
He wished that he had quit before, with only one disgrace.
"I'm hopeless as a runner now; I shouldn't try to race."
But, in the distant crowd he searched, and found his father's face.
That steady look, which said again, "Get up - and win the race!"
So up he jumped to try again, ten yards behind the last.
If I'm going to gain those yards, he thought, I've got to do it fast.
Exerting everything he had, he picked up eight or ten,
But trying so hard to catch the lead, he slipped and fell again.

Defeat - he lay there silently, a tear dropped from his eye.
There's just no sense in running now - three strikes; I'm out; why try?
The will to rise had disappeared, all hope had fled away.
So far behind, so error prone, a loser all the way.
I've lost, so what's the use, he thought. I'll live with my disgrace.
But then he thought about his dad, who soon he'd have to

BECOMING WHEALTHY

face.

Get up, an echo sounded low. You haven't lost at all.
For winning is no more than this - To rise each time you fall.
So, up he rose, to win once more, and with a new commit,
Resolved that - either win or lose - at least he wouldn't quit.
So far behind the others now, the most he'd ever been,
Still, he gave it all he had, and ran as though to win.
Three times he'd fallen stumbling; three times he rose again.
Too far behind to hope to win, he still ran to the end.

They cheered the winning runner as he finished in first place,
Head high and proud and happy; no falling, no disgrace.
But when the fallen youngster crossed the finish line - last place,
The crowd gave him the greater cheer, for finishing the race.
And, even though he came in last, with head bowed low, unproud,
You would have thought he'd won the race, to listen to the crowd.
And to his dad he sadly said, "I didn't do so well."
"To me, you won", his father said. "You rose each time you fell."

And when things seem too dark and hard and difficult to face,
The memory of that little boy helps keep me in the race.
For all of life is like that race, with ups and downs and all.
And all you have to do to win, is rise each time you fall.

BECOMING WHEALTHY

There are several definitions for *inspire*, the root word for inspiration. Since the root word for inspire is *spirit*, some definitions of inspire stray from its original definition. The closest definition to fit the case of "The Race" is probably "to fill with noble or reverent emotion". Most of the other definitions for inspire use terms like "arouse by divine influence," "stimulate to creativity or action," or "to bring about a cause of action".

Christopher McDougall's excellent book, *Born to Run*, chronicles the Tarahumara people of Mexico, who routinely hold races of fifty to one hundred miles for the sheer love of running. The book also introduces us to several Americans who are deeply into running these ultra-marathons. These people are several standard deviations from the norm in almost every respect.

One of these super-runners is Jenn "Mookie" Shelton, a twenty-something who might be mislabeled a slacker, if not for her incredibly energy for living on the edge. The author emphasizes that living on the edge isn't about danger; it's about curiosity, audacious curiosity, the kind that brings inspiration. Jenn and her partner Billy's inspiration is summed up as follows: "They were expected to accomplish nothing, so they could try anything. Audacity beckoned." Sometimes inspiration is the result of realizing you have nothing to lose.

A photo of Jenn appeared in a running magazine after she became a world-ranked ultra-marathoner. She was finishing a 30-mile race in the Virginia backwoods. McDougall's description of the photo of Jenn smiling and running is also an inspiring description of the beauty and power of inspiration itself:

BECOMING WHEALTHY

"...that smile is strangely stirring. You can tell she's having an absolute blast, as if there's nothing on earth she'd rather be doing and nowhere on earth she'd rather be doing it than here, on this lost trail in the middle of the Appalachian wilderness. Even though she's just run four miles farther than a marathon, she looks light-footed and care-free, her eyes twinkling, her ponytail swinging around her head like a shirt in the fist of a triumphant Brazilian soccer player. Her naked delight is unmistakable; it forces a smile to her lips that's so honest and unguarded, you feel she's lost in the grip of <u>artistic inspiration</u>."

My favorite definition of *inspire* is "to breathe life into." This definition has medical connotations, though it transcends the purely medical. This definition also makes it clearer that *inspire* is the opposite of *expire*, which in medical terms means to die. To be inspired, then, is the beginning of life for whatever you're inspired to do. By implication, when you are not inspired to do something, eventually that something will expire. First, we have inspiration; then to keep the spirit alive, we have respiration. Finally, without respiration, we have expiration.

When you are inspired to do something, you are pulled toward it, not pushed toward it. There is an irresistible draw to create something more than currently exists.

Our most noble professions are given a term that is not bestowed on more mundane occupations. That term is *calling*. Calling is most closely associated with religious vocations, but a vocation can be any occupation to which one feels drawn. Most callings and vocations have something in common - their primary purpose is to serve others. Those with a true calling in any profession not only become the most successful in that profession, but they are also sought out above others for their services.

You would not seek out a doctor who was in it for the prestige or money. You would not seek out a priest who was in it for the power. You would not seek out a teacher for your child who was in it for the summer vacations. You want to know that the main reason those people are in those professions is because they were called into them by the opportunity to make life better for people like you.

When you're inspired, you have to channel a seemingly endless source of energy. Your body may tire, but your spirit never does. Rather than feeling like a donkey who is being prodded forward with a stick (and maybe a carrot), you feel like a dog who is tugging at the leash to run to the next adventure. To use another analogy, when you are inspired, you may not always know the best way to position the rudder, but your sails are always full.

When you're inspired, you find yourself thinking of ways to channel that passion to get the most out of it. When you're inspired, your passion becomes more than what you do - it becomes a large part of who you are. It also feels effortless.

We spend more waking hours working than on any other activity over our lifetimes. Work provides most, if not all of our income, which is usually the primary, if not the sole source of wealth. The time and demands of our work also have an enormous impact on our health. Even those jobs that are not physically demanding may be highly stressful. The time demands of work often steal time from activities like sleep and exercise, resulting in much poorer health.

Anyone who has ever taken a psychology course is familiar with Maslow's Hierarchy of Needs. Abraham Maslow developed his theory in 1943. The hierarchy is, in descending order:
- **Self-Actualization** (morality, creativity, spontaneity)
- **Esteem** (achievement, confidence, respect from others)
- **Love/Belonging** (friendship, family, sexual intimacy)
- **Safety** (physical security, employment, health, family)
- **Physiological** (breathing, food, water, sleep, sex)

Maslow theorized that, until one's needs are met at the lower levels, one cannot or will not devote energy to meeting needs at the higher levels. This assumption is valid - you can't focus on your job if you haven't had enough sleep or food; you can't focus on friendships if you are about to lose your job; you can't focus on becoming a more well-rounded person when a loved one is battling a life-threatening disease. The hierarchy of needs is one way of measuring how well we are achieving our full potential.

There is a similar hierarchy when we look at our work. If you are out of work, it can become a desperate struggle just to meet the physiological needs at the bottom of the hierarchy. When you do get a job, you hope it will pay enough to meet your physiological needs. You seek to stay with an employer and hopefully get some raises and promotions in order to fulfill your safety needs. However, when a job is just a job, it won't provide much more than these basic needs. Because these jobs neither demand much nor provide much, you may put your back into it, but not your heart and soul.

Most people aspire to have more than a job - they want a career. A career is a series of jobs that enables you to move up on the hierarchy of needs. A career will usually enable you to buy more of the things that people seek on the lower level of needs. The most attractive aspect of a career is that it offers the opportunity to fulfill our esteem needs.

If you're lucky, a job leads to a career. If you're luckier, your career becomes your vocation. A vocation is defined as an occupation or profession for which a person is especially suited or qualified. Someone who merely works in a job may be a square peg in a round hole. Someone who builds a career is likely to be a square peg in a square hole, though more careers are made by reshaping a round peg into a square one than by reshaping a square hole into a round one. With a vocation, you are not only a square peg in a square hole; you are the right size peg for that hole.

Finally, we have the pinnacle of the work hierarchy, the calling. We often think of callings in terms of religions, but a calling can be for any work that benefits others primarily and the worker secondarily. A calling is not work that one does for selfish reasons.

When you merely have a job, you do the job for the pay. If there is any non-monetary benefit to the job, it won't keep you from leaving for a modest raise elsewhere. With a career, there are benefits beyond pay, but you are unlikely to change careers if you could not make as much money in another career, even if you enjoyed the work more.

When you have a vocation, you continuously find it hard to believe that you actually get paid to do something you love. You are not about to give up the financial benefits, but they begin to assume secondary importance to what you receive beyond the paycheck.

Finally, a calling is work that you would pay money to others for the privilege of performing. You are so drawn to do that work, and you are so called by that work that it doesn't matter what you have to do in order to work in that field - you will do it. With a vocation, a person usually starts out with a skill set that makes that vocation a rewarding and easy choice. With a calling, a skill set may have to be acquired through years of training, and even then it might not be enough.

When viewed through the prism of Maslow's Hierarchy of Needs, most jobs take a bottom-up approach. The job promises to provide money in exchange for work, and that money can be used to supply one's basic needs. The reason most people can't get passionate about their jobs is that the job doesn't provide an opportunity to release their passions. Without passion for your work, the most you are likely to become in that work is "competent", which means you are capable of competing (but not necessarily winning).

A calling takes a top-down approach regarding the hierarchy of needs. A calling speaks to something inside the individual that promises to make them a better person, typically by providing the opportunity for that person to make the world a better place. A calling will provide you with the needs at the top of the hierarchy first. The more basic of needs get met as the effect of being passionate about the work leads to being more than competent in performing it. By excellently providing something of value to people, they then provide the means to meet all the basic needs.

Becoming whealthy requires a top-down approach to Maslow's Hierarchy of Needs. The reason I've discussed jobs, careers, vocations, and callings to this extent is that it is important to understand that the lower levels focus on feeding the purse alone. They can often do that at the expense of the body and the mind. At the lower levels, there is no feeding of the soul; at most one can hope that the soul isn't being harmed by one's work, which is not to say that there is no value to work that provides only a paycheck.

The work you would most want to do, the work that you would do for no pay, the work that never seems like work, that work is your calling. It may be possible to transform your current job into your calling, but it's a tough job working from the bottom up to make such a change.

I also don't recommend you quit your job, pitch a tent in the woods, and contemplate your true calling for the next year. I recommend you first look at your current situation and see if there is the potential to transform your job into a calling, to be pulled rather than pushed into getting up each day and going to work. In the meantime, do some soul-searching to ask yourself what kind of work you could do that:
a) would give you a sense of purpose;
b) would be within your capabilities at some point;
c) would enable you to meet your more basic needs as well.
It might take years to find your true calling, but the first step in finding your true calling is to realize you have one and to begin looking for it.

People are inspired to greatness; they are almost never motivated to it. Remember, inspiration pulls you; motivation pushes you. It's just too exhausting to be pushed all the way to greatness. If you're merely motivated by family, friends, peers, greed, fear, competitors, enemies, or a thousand other "motivating factors," you may achieve greatness, but it will feel empty and, more importantly, it will be fleeting. Greatness built on motivation without inspiration is like a foundation that is made with concrete that has too much sand and not enough cement. It may look solid, but time quickly exposes the weakness, and whatever was built on that foundation soon collapses.

The first, best way to become whealthy is to become inspired in your work. Your work can be whatever you define it to be; it doesn't have to be something you do for pay, although almost everything we do for pay is classified as work. For most of us, work is the primary, if not the sole, source of income. Work occupies more waking hours than any other single activity for almost everyone who works full-time.

For better or worse, much of our identity is connected to our work. When you meet someone for the first time, one of the very first questions most people ask is "What do you do for a living?" The work environment has a tremendous effect on our physical, mental, and emotional health. When work is going well, we feel strong, confident, and exhilarated. More often, though, work creates physical, mental, and emotional stress that damages our health in ways that might not become evident for years.

If you remember reading Mark Twain's *The Adventures of Tom Sawyer* in school, you may recall Tom using psychology to get his friend Ben to whitewash the fence for him, a task that Tom despised doing. Tom seduced Ben to take over the task by acting as though he loved to whitewash and that he didn't think Ben was capable of doing the job properly:

"He had discovered a great law of human action, without knowing it – namely, that in order to make a

man or a boy covet a thing, it is only necessary to make the thing difficult to attain. If he had been a great and wise philosopher, like the writer of this book, he would now have comprehended that Work consists of whatever a body is obliged to do, and that Play consists of whatever a body is not obliged to do."

Have you ever donated blood? The good feeling that one gets from donating blood is something that can't be put into monetary terms. Research has shown that when blood donors are offered financial compensation, their donations *decrease*. People don't want to have their good deed cheapened by someone putting a price tag on it. Monetary motivation doesn't work because blood donors are giving and receiving something that money can't buy.

Wikipedia has been proven to be at least as accurate as conventional encyclopedias compiled by experts. Encyclopedias from Microsoft's *Encarta* to *Encyclopedia Britannica* have gone out of business. The best encyclopedias that could be put together by professionals have been usurped by a free online encyclopedia that is put together by millions of amateurs.

There are two factors that explain the success of Wikipedia. The first one is the recognition by Wikipedia's creators that none of us is as smart as all of us. The second is that when people are interested in something, they don't have to be enticed to share their interest with others.

These three examples of Tom Sawyer, blood donations, and Wikipedia share a common element - they show how people can be motivated to do something for free that logic contends would require payment as an incentive since some people do, or did, the same things for money.

There is a fundamental reason why money doesn't work as well as a motivator as most people might think. Money doesn't work as a motivator in practice as well as in theory because we have a tendency to think of money as the cause, as the motivator, if you will. Money isn't the cause of our work; it's the effect.

Frederick Herzberg was an American psychologist who greatly influenced business management with what is generally referred to as the Two-Factor Theory. Herzberg's theory states that people are not content with satisfaction at the lower levels of Maslow's hierarchy of needs. Individuals will also seek gratification of higher-level psychological needs related to achievement, recognition, responsibility, advancement, and the nature of the work itself.

Two-factor theory distinguishes between:
- **Motivators** (challenging work, recognition, responsibility, achievement) that give positive satisfaction arising from intrinsic conditions of the work itself and
- **Hygiene factors** (status, job security, salary, fringe benefits, work conditions) that do not give positive satisfaction, though their absence results in dissatisfaction. These factors are extrinsic to the work itself.

Essentially, hygiene factors are necessary to prevent an employee from becoming dissatisfied. Motivation factors are needed to motivate an employee to higher performance. Herzberg further classified workers' actions and how and why they do them. If you perform a work-related action because you *have* to, then that is classed as movement; if you perform a work-related action because you *want* to, then that is classed as motivation.

At some time in his youth, Frederick Herzberg probably read *The Adventures of Tom Sawyer*. Herzberg made a career and influenced business management practices by quantitatively proving what Mark Twain said - work consists of what you have to do and play consists of what you want to do.

What is the environment where you work? If the hygiene factors are lacking or inadequate, it can be hard for you to feel anything but dissatisfied. In such an environment, morale is low, turnover is high, and businesses that don't provide a minimum level of hygiene factors don't stay in business for long.

When a business is just starting up, the environment may be one where the hygiene factors are low, but the motivators are high. Hygiene factors are low because money is tight in most start-ups. The company can't offer security yet, but what they can offer is plenty of opportunity. It can be an exciting environment where everyone is excited about the prospect of building something from scratch as a team. That enthusiasm and dedication should translate into profits at some point, and at that point the employer needs to raise the hygiene factors to an acceptable level.

Old school business thinking was that as long as the business took care of the hygiene factors, it was up to the employees to find their own motivation. If management focused more on people than numbers, an unproductive environment could result. The main reason people stay in such jobs is that the hygiene factors there are better than the hygiene factors elsewhere. People get used to a certain level of salaries and benefits, and they are reluctant to give some of that up for intangibles like recognition and achievement.

The goal is to have a work environment that offers both the requisite level of hygiene factors and as many motivators as possible. What many business managers fail to recognize is that the way to get workers to be their most productive is to pay them enough that money is not an issue (which does not mean paying them more than anyone else or paying the employee as much as they demand) and then to provide as many motivators as possible.

To help get the proper perspective of money as a motivator, consider this situation. At your place of employment, you feel you are well-paid for the work you do. However, you just found out that two of your co-workers, neither of whom is more productive than you are, both earn more than you do. Would that news make you suddenly dissatisfied with your level of pay? What if you found out that those two co-workers were more satisfied with their jobs than you are, based on a survey all the workers completed? Would you care? That bit of information would be unlikely to raise your level of dissatisfaction.

The situation just described illustrates a point - the best motivators are the ones that have no limits. When someone finds out that co-workers are paid more, they become dissatisfied because they believe that others' higher income must come at their own expense. When someone finds out that co-workers are more satisfied in their jobs, they do not become dissatisfied because satisfaction is not a finite resource; it can be created in infinite quantities by those who will benefit most from its creation.

BECOMING WHEALTHY

We tend to think of those hygiene factors as motivators in part because of the Industrial Revolution. Before the Industrial Revolution, work was arduous and often dangerous, but for the most part it wasn't routine. Two-thirds of the population worked in agriculture prior to the Industrial Revolution. That work had many drawbacks, but at least there was a certain variety to it.

Prior to the Industrial Revolution, there were no assembly lines. With the advent of the modern factory, tasks were broken down to their smallest elements, and workers would perform those smallest elements continuously. If you worked at a Ford assembly plant in 1920, you could take pride that you were part of the team that built the Model T, the car that put America on wheels. However, your workday consisted of attaching the front bumper on the driver's side as each car came down the line. By the end of the year, you would have attached 171,428 bumpers to 171,428 Model T's. Work like that required a lot of outside direction and supervision. No one can stay self-motivated performing the same routine 86 times an hour, 8 hours a day, 250 days a year.

Non-routine jobs are far more common today. The pace of change requires that jobs evolve continuously to keep up with new technologies and competition. The push for productivity now has workers multi-tasking, as opposed to breaking work down into smaller and smaller increments. The variety of activities in the average workday today makes it easier for workers to maintain interest in their work. The number of workers putting in 10 and 12 hour workdays may be the result of the push for more productivity, but they could not be productive for 10 or 12 hours a day unless the work was able to hold their interest for that long a period.

One of the great motivators is autonomy. We all want to think we are the ones who decide what we are going to do. If you are a parent, you have probably used an If-Then scenario with your child at some time. They can be stated positively or negatively, as a carrot or a stick: "If you clean your room, we can go get ice cream. If you don't clean your room, you can't play any video games." If-Then rewards, and especially punishments, are perceived as reducing one's autonomy.

Autonomy is one of those intrinsic motivators. Intrinsic motivators are delicate things. They can be damaged by, of all things, extrinsic rewards. Bobby Jones was one of the greatest golfers of all time, winning thirteen major tournaments. He also co-founded Augusta National and the Masters Tournament. He was a lawyer by profession and only played golf as an amateur. When asked why he never turned pro, he replied, "When you play for money, it's not love anymore." The lesson of Bobby Jones is: when people are doing something because of intrinsic motivators, don't muck it up by offering extrinsic rewards. You will only hurt their performance.

Extrinsic rewards, like money, can send two seemingly contradictory signals at the same time. The first signal is that the task you are performing is valuable and that someone wants to demonstrate appreciation of you performing it with financial compensation. The second signal is that the task you are performing is inherently undesirable and that the only way to entice you to perform this undesirable task is to offer you financial compensation. We prefer the first signal simply because there is an intrinsic element to it: the recognition and appreciation of our performing a task well.

Extrinsic rewards, like money, tend to have a more addictive quality, compared to intrinsic rewards. We easily get used to whatever level of material comfort we currently enjoy, a trait known as adaptation. If we suddenly had to take a pay cut of 10%, we would experience symptoms similar to drug withdrawal. We are capable of adapting to the change for the worse, but we certainly don't like it; furthermore, it clouds our attitude toward our work. Also, once we get paid for doing something, it's unlikely we will ever be willing to do it again for free. In such a case, we are willing to give up the good vibes of doing something for the joy of it if we are no longer getting paid to do it. It feels as if we are giving away something of value to someone who should be paying for it.

In order to feel motivated, we need to feel that the work we are performing has some importance, and we also need to feel a certain sense of urgency about it. A sense of urgency and importance isn't hard to come by if you're the attending physician in a hospital emergency room; it may be harder to generate those feelings when you're reviewing expense reports at your company.

There's a reason why every task at work needs to be done. If you don't see how your task fits into the big picture at work, you owe it to yourself to find out how the work you do makes a positive difference in people's lives. Your boss, if he/she is worthy of the position, knows you deserve such knowledge and that such knowledge can be a great motivator.

Your boss should also recognize that once you feel a sense of urgency and importance to your work, the best thing to do is free you to get the work done in the best way you see fit. If you are properly motivated about the purpose of your work, you are also properly motivated to do that work to the best of your ability and as efficiently as possible.

Self-determination theory (SDT) is a theory of motivation developed by Edward L. Deci and Richard M. Ryan at the University of Rochester in the 1980's. SDT contends that humans have three innate psychological needs - competence, autonomy, and relatedness. The three needs cited in SDT can be defined as follows:

- **Competence**: to seek to control the outcome and experience mastery of a task
- **Autonomy**: the universal urge to be the causal agent of one's own life and to act in harmony with one's integrated self, though this action does not mean to be independent of others
- **Relatedness**: the universal desire to interact, be connected to, and experience caring for others

From the Self-Determination Theory web site:

"Within SDT, the nutriments for healthy development and functioning are specified using the concept of basic psychological needs for autonomy, competence, and relatedness. **To the extent that the needs are ongoingly satisfied, people will develop and function effectively and experience wellness, but to the extent that they are thwarted, people more likely evidence ill-being and non-optimal functioning.** *The darker sides of human behavior and experience, such as certain types of psychopathology, prejudice, and aggression are understood in terms of reactions to basic needs having been thwarted, either developmentally or proximally."* (emphasis mine)

Deci and Ryan's studies quantified that people who have their intrinsic needs met on the job are both healthier and, just as important, perform better over time, leading to higher compensation and more wealth. Those who focused on extrinsic rewards, especially money alone, felt more stress, felt less fulfillment, and, in the long run, had less success, and earned less than their counterparts who focused on intrinsic rewards and let the money take care of itself. Deci and Ryan and others who have followed have shown conclusively that when you recognize that money is not the cause, but the effect, you end up with more money, and you are far happier on the way to attaining it.

More and more people are pursuing Master's degrees these days. Some are in programs because the job market isn't good for them. Some know they need more than a Bachelor's degree to be competitive in their field. Almost all of them seek what is implied by the title of the degree - they seek mastery of a subject.

As we have become more and more specialized in our jobs, mastery of the skills needed to perform our jobs has become more and more critical to our success. To be a jack of all trades is to be, by default in this era, a master of none. All trades require a level of mastery that makes it almost impossible for the average person to excel in more than a few areas.

We instinctively want to become highly skilled in a field for two important reasons. First, higher skill levels lead to higher compensation - ask any professional athlete. Second - and this reason is more important for most people - mastery leads to greater autonomy. Mastery of your work skills leads to mastery of your life.

When a job challenges us beyond our skill levels, we feel stressed. When a job doesn't challenge us at all, we become bored and disengaged. When we are challenged enough that we are fully engaged without being stressed, we are said to be in flow, or in sports parlance, in the zone. There is a sweet spot each of us has where we are energized by the challenge of our work, instead of being either debilitated or disinterested by it.

Because we have a tendency to get bored easily, mastery becomes a moving target. The rapid pace of change necessitates that we all continually upgrade our skills to remain competitive in the workforce. However, this rapid pace of change creates an externally imposed mandate to upgrade one's skills, which we are learning is a poor way to motivate people. We also have an intrinsic desire to upgrade our skills, in part because we don't want to become complacent and bored in our work, but also because mastery feels good, and continuous improvement is the best way to maintain that good feeling.

It is never necessary to *be the best*; it is only necessary to *do your best*. (When you do your best, you will occasionally be the best, too.) Being the best is another one of those extrinsic factors - you are basing your mastery on a comparison to others. Because you can't control the skills and talents of others, you end up ceding your happiness and sense of worth to something beyond your control.

Doing your best puts all the control with you, where it belongs. You set the standard; you do the evaluating; you hand out the rewards. And true mastery involves a commitment that, however good you are at something today, your goal is to be a little better tomorrow.

When it comes to undertaking any project, we are quick to ask who-what-when-where-how questions. In our haste to get those questions answered in order to tackle the task at hand, we often fail to ask the most important question - why.

Asking, and more importantly, being able to give a proper answer to the question of why you are doing something is the entire key to motivation. No one is motivated by who-what-when-where-how questions. They are only motivated by the answer to the why question. Before you can delve into the mechanics of becoming whealthy, you have to be able to give a satisfactory question as to why you want to become whealthy.

Answering the question of why is rarely as easy as it seems, at least if you try to do it right. In the matter of becoming whealthy, you are attempting to attain two things - wealth and health - that you claim to want very badly, at least badly enough to be reading this book. Yet your goal has eluded you so far. There may be problems with the who-what-when-where-how part of your plan, and we will address much of that in later chapters. Right now the question before you is why do you want to become whealthy?

How you answer why you want to become whealthy will determine how successful you will be at actually becoming whealthy. Becoming whealthy will almost certainly require some major changes in how you conduct your life on a day-to-day basis. These changes will require some serious effort on your part.

As you contemplate the reasons why you want to become whealthy, it's a good idea to write those reasons down. As you compile your reasons why you want to become whealthy, break them into three categories: selfless, self-interest, and selfish. Selfless means that only others will benefit and that you will likely make some sacrifice. Self-interest is not selfish; it means your actions are likely to benefit you without harming others. Selfish means only you benefit and others will likely sacrifice.

You will have to determine which category each reason falls into. If you aren't sure which category to select, select the less altruistic one. If you give a reason a more altruistic rating than it deserves, that reason is likely to disappoint you as a source of motivation.

Here is an example of categorizing your reasons. You may have a goal to lose thirty pounds. A selfless reason to lose the weight would be the fear that the weight will lead to a heart attack and might leave you unable to provide an income to support your children. A self-interest reason would be the opportunity to get a lower premium on health insurance by moving into a more preferred rating class. A selfish reason would be the desire to be on the receiving end of longing looks the next time you're at the beach, making your partner jealous.

If there are multiple reasons for working toward something, the chances are greater that you will achieve success, assuming at least some of those reasons are not selfish. Selfish reasons can only motivate for brief periods. When the expected payoff proves disappointing, a new motivation becomes necessary. Multiple reasons can offer a safety net when willpower weakens.

Ultimately, the more selfless reasons are the ones that motivate people long term; the selfish reasons can be a nice bonus. The desire to lose weight to remain healthy and live long enough to give your children the parent they need is a good enough reason. Looking hot at the beach is a nice bonus, though.

Motivation is more like respiration than inspiration. Motivation doesn't get us breathing, but it can help keep us breathing when breathing gets difficult.

When we are trying to do something positive, it can help to focus on the long term gain instead of the short term pain. When we are trying to avoid doing something negative, like giving in to an addiction, trying to think long term can create a seemingly impossible burden. If an alcoholic thinks in terms of "I'm *never* going to drink again," the pressure to keep such a promise is sure to break his/her will. Thinking in terms of "I'm not going to drink *today*" reduces the commitment to a level that feels manageable. Also, since we inhabit only the present, it is the only time period we can, or need to, keep under our control.

Even when you're inspired, you still need motivation. Inspiration helps you produce a strategy; motivation helps you develop tactics. The best way to get and stay motivated is to find a cause that is bigger than just you.

We generally work harder to prevent disappointing others than to prevent disappointing ourselves. Look for intrinsic reasons to do something. Make the effort because it affects you in positive, intangible ways, not because others think you should do it or because someone or something is prodding you with carrots and sticks.

Finally, make sure you answer the why question before you worry about answering who-what-when-where-how questions. The proper answer to the why question will provide inspiration *and* keep you motivated. When you properly answer the why question, you will also find a lot of who-what-when-where-how questions begin to answer themselves.

Becoming CONNECTED

MENDING WALL by Robert Frost

Something there is that doesn't love a wall,
That sends the frozen-ground-swell under it,
And spills the upper boulders in the sun,
And makes gaps even two can pass abreast.
The work of hunters is another thing:
I have come after them and made repair
Where they have left not one stone on a stone,
But they would have the rabbit out of hiding,
To please the yelping dogs. The gaps I mean,
No one has seen them made or heard them made,
But at spring mending-time we find them there.
I let my neighbor know beyond the hill;
And on a day we meet to walk the line
And set the wall between us once again.
We keep the wall between us as we go.
To each the boulders that have fallen to each.
And some are loaves and some so nearly balls
We have to use a spell to make them balance:
"Stay where you are until our backs are turned!"
We wear our fingers rough with handling them.
Oh, just another kind of outdoor game,
One on a side. It comes to little more.
There where it is we do not need the wall:
He is all pine and I am apple orchard.
My apple trees will never get across
And eat the cones under his pines, I tell him.
He only says, "Good fences make good neighbors."
Spring is the mischief in me, and I wonder

BECOMING WHEALTHY

If I could put a notion in his head:
"Why do they make good neighbors?"
Isn't it where there are cows?
But here there are no cows.
Before I built a wall I'd ask to know
What I was walling in or walling out,
And to whom I was like to give offense.
Something there is that doesn't love a wall,
That wants it down. I could say 'Elves' to him,
But it's not elves exactly, and I'd rather
He said it for himself. I see him there
Bringing a stone grasped firmly by the top
In each hand, like an old-stone savage armed.
He moves in darkness as it seems to me;
Not of woods only and the shade of trees.
He will not go behind his father's saying,
And he likes having thought of it so well.
He says again, "Good fences make good neighbors."

Because I am a financial planner, most people think that my work is centered on money. My work is not centered on money - it is centered on people. Money is merely a tool that people use to help them fulfill their needs and wants.

In recent years, my research has dealt more with psychology that finance. My work isn't about money; it's about our *relationship* with money, which means I need to understand as much about how people work as I do about how money works.

All humans share one common goal - we all seek happiness. Happiness means different things to different people. Even people who have a similar concept of happiness might seek that happiness in very different ways. One of the frustrations of being human is how badly we can misjudge what we think will make us happy.

Many, if not most people believe that more money will make them happy. Studies conducted in many countries over several decades have reached some interesting conclusions. First, if you are living in poverty, it is harder to be happy, though many do succeed. Second, once you reach the average income for your society, the additional happiness from more money is marginal. Third, the sacrifices made to substantially increase one's income above the average can lead to unhappiness and regret.

Wealth has been found not to be the source of happiness. People who attain wealth find that out eventually, and a large portion of humanity spends their lives seeking it in vain.

Health is an area that tends to bring unhappiness, but not necessarily happiness. When we are in good physical health, we tend to take it for granted, more than we take good financial health for granted. It is only when we are not in good health that we have a proper appreciation for it.

Bronnie Ware is an Australian nurse who spent several years working in palliative care, caring for patients in the last 12 weeks of their lives. She recorded their dying epiphanies, writing of the phenomenal clarity of vision that people gain at the end of their lives and of how we might learn from their wisdom. "When questioned about any regrets they had or anything they would do differently," she says, "common themes surfaced again and again."

Here are the top five regrets of the dying, as witnessed by Ware:

BECOMING WHEALTHY

1. I wish I'd had the courage to live a life true to myself, not the life others expected of me.
"When people realize that their life is almost over and look back clearly on it, it is easy to see how many dreams have gone unfulfilled. Most people had to die knowing that it was due to choices they had made."

2. I wish I hadn't worked so hard.
"This came from every male patient that I nursed. They missed their children's youth and their partner's companionship. All of the men I nursed deeply regretted spending so much of their lives on the treadmill of a work existence."

3. I wish I'd had the courage to express my feelings.
"Many people suppressed their feelings in order to keep peace with others. As a result, they settled for a mediocre existence and never became who they were truly capable of becoming."

4. I wish I had stayed in touch with my friends.
"Often they would not truly realize the full benefits of old friends until their dying weeks and it was not always possible to track them down. There were many deep regrets about not giving friendships the time and effort that they deserved."

5. I wish that I had let myself be happier.
"This is a surprisingly common one. Many did not realize until the end that happiness is a choice."

A person's level of happiness is directly correlated with his/her level of social interaction. The more friends you have and the deeper those friendships are, the happier you are likely to be.

Americans put a high value on individualism, but we rarely take a close look at the price of individualism. We may view past emphasis on faith, family, community, and country as stifling. But focusing on "we" first and "I" second got Americans through the Great Depression and World War II, and it built the great economic superpower we became after the war. It's hard to get through tough times when you feel an "I", rather than part of a "we."

Viktor Frankl was a rising star in the field of psychiatry in the early 1940's, until he was swept up in a roundup of Jews in Vienna in 1942 and sent to Auschwitz and later to Dachau concentration camps. While in those camps, he developed the basis for what would become one of the most important books of the twentieth century, *Man's Search for Meaning*.

The core of Frankl's work is his contention that "man's main concern is not to gain pleasure or avoid pain, but rather to see a meaning in his life." Frankl also knew that meaning did not come from money: "People have enough to live, but nothing to live for; they have the means but no meaning."

In the camps, Frankl observed that those who focused on helping others survive, rather than focusing on their own considerable agony, were less likely to give up and die. In one of his most moving passages, Frankl writes, "I understand how a man who has nothing left in the world still may know bliss, be it only for a brief moment, in the contemplation of his beloved."

People become members of a church for two reasons - to strengthen their connection to God and to strengthen their connection to other people. People who are involved in some form of organized religion have fewer health problems, fewer financial problems, longer lives, and higher measures of happiness than their non-religious counterparts. Some of these benefits are the result of trusting in a higher power to see them through life's crises. They are also the result of having a support system of people who can offer a helping hand, a pat on the back, and even a kick in the butt as the situation requires.

In the late nineteenth century, sociologist Emile Durkheim gathered data from across Europe to study factors that affect the suicide rate. No matter how Durkheim parsed the data, one fact never changed - the fewer social bonds, constraints, and obligations a person had, the higher the risk for suicide. People with the less demanding religious lives had higher suicide rates. People living alone were most likely to take their own life; married people, less; married people with children, still less.

A century of studies since Durkheim have confirmed his findings. Having strong social networks strengthens your immune system, extends life expectancy (even more than quitting smoking), speeds recovery from illness and injury, and reduces the risks of depression and anxiety disorders. If you want to be healthy, good friends may be the best medicine.

Animals with bigger brains have more complex social networks, and we humans are at the top of that list. We have large frontal lobes because we have the largest social groups. We have the largest social groups because we could not survive without them. We did not become the dominant species on the planet because of any purely physical superiority. The only way we survived as a species, much less came to dominate, was because of our ability to develop and maintain complex social networks. What has worked for us as a species for thousands of years also applies to us as individuals. The better we are at developing connections with other people, the better our chances for survival, success, and ultimately, happiness.

Social networks are excellent at offering support when we need it. They are also excellent at providing constraints when we need those, too. There are the obvious examples, such as judicial systems that discourage criminal behavior that is detrimental to the group.

Social networks help us stay on task when we make a commitment to positive change. If you tell all your Facebook friends that you are going to lose ten pounds in the next two months, you know you will have to provide an accounting to them at the end of the period.

The term social network is appropriate in certain circumstances. What we really need involves more than the typical social network, certainly more than one can get from social media, no matter how many Facebook friends you have. What we really need are relationship support systems where the bonds to others are both strong and interconnected.

Ambrose Bierce, the nineteenth century journalist, defined an acquaintance as "someone we know well enough to borrow from, but not well enough to lend to." The networks of greatest value are those that are comprised of more than acquaintances. You need people from whom you can borrow, but more important, you need people to whom you are willing to lend.

These deeper relationship networks not only provide a sense of belonging and moral support, they also provide the opportunity to feel needed, which may be the most important benefit of all. When we get older, we often lose the connections that made us feel needed. Our children grow up and move away. We retire from our jobs. Our spouses may pass away. One of the reasons why volunteerism is strongest among those over 65 is the need they have to still feel needed.

Our ability to establish and maintain relationships is not unlimited. In fact, anthropologists have calculated that, throughout human history, we tend to peak out at about 150 when it comes to relationships that go beyond mere acquaintances. The number of significant relationships a person has is similar, regardless of geography or culture.

The similar pattern of relationships across humanity has led anthropologists to the *village theory*. This group of 150 or so individuals who comprise our significant relationships is our "village." These people may be spread out over time and space, but they are the group with whom almost all of our serious human interactions occur.

The best relationships are built on five attributes: respect, shared experience, mutual enjoyment of each other's company, trust, and reciprocity. The ability to establish and maintain all five of these attributes in a relationship is one reason why the number of meaningful relationships we can handle is limited. The importance of a relationship in our lives is also based largely on to what degree these five attributes are present.

When we are free to choose a relationship, the ability to respect someone is one of the first requirements. If we don't respect someone, it's unlikely we will want to establish any kind of relationship. Some relationships that are established for us, such as with our parents, assume a level of respect. Once we have the option of discontinuing such a relationship, the respect must be earned. The loss of respect for a person can be an instant relationship killer, such as when we discover a friend has been cheating on a spouse or a business partner.

Shared experiences bond people together, especially if the experience is profoundly positive or negative. A profoundly positive experience is something on the order of bringing a child into the world together, not merely taking a cruise together. Experiences that involved hardship, danger, or suffering are often the catalyst for our deepest friendships. Many a lifelong friend has been made on the battlefield. Misery truly does love company.

We want to have relationships when we enjoy spending time with each other. However, we have to spend a lot of time with people whose company we don't particularly enjoy. Such situations are especially true at work, where we don't get to choose our co-workers. The people with whom we want to spend time are those who share some of our interests. They also possess enough social skills to make their presence something to be enjoyed, rather than merely tolerated.

Along with respect, trust must be present at the beginning of a relationship, or it is unlikely to form. Trust is greatest where the relationship is deepest. If a casual friend failed to keep a piece of shared gossip secret, the relationship would lose value, even though we might not feel compelled to end the relationship. On the other hand, if we found out our spouse had been unfaithful, a betrayal of trust on that level by someone that close is almost certain to irreparably damage the relationship.

Even in the strongest, most enduring, and most noble of relationships, certain rules, mostly unspoken, still apply. In order to maintain the relationship and reap its benefits, it is necessary to abide by these codes.

As a social construct, *reciprocity* means that in response to friendly actions, people are frequently much nicer and much more cooperative than what could be expected by the self-interest model. Conversely, in response to hostile actions, reciprocity is frequently much nastier and sometimes quite brutal. Reciprocity encompasses the concepts of the Golden Rule, mutual back scratching, quid pro quo, and an eye for an eye.

Reciprocity is not the same as altruism or even gift giving. Altruism is helping those less fortunate, with the only reward being the positive feelings that result from the good deed. Gift giving is not typically based on need, but rather on the desire to make someone else happy. When a grandparent gives a gift to a grandchild, neither altruism nor reciprocity is a factor in that action.

Reciprocity is based both on the other party's intentions as well as the consequences of their actions. We actually feel a greater obligation to reciprocate when someone attempts to do us a favor that doesn't work out than we do for someone who inadvertently benefits us. Reciprocity is based on a trading of favors, as opposed to a formal negotiation or contract.

In addition to positive reciprocity, there is also negative reciprocity, which might be construed as retaliation or revenge. Negative reciprocity, unlike positive reciprocity, doesn't have the expectation of gain. Other than the pleasure of getting back at someone who has harmed you, the only other benefit to negative reciprocity may be to discourage such acts in the future. In certain circles, such as the Mafia, to not retaliate when you've been wronged is taken as a sign of weakness and invites even worse abuses in the future.

BECOMING WHEALTHY

One problem of reciprocity focuses on the unequal profit obtained from the concept of reciprocal concessions. The emotional burden to repay bothers some more than others, causing some to overcompensate with more than what was given originally. People who want something from us know that the best way to get it is to give us something that is unsolicited (and of lower value) first, and then wait for the reciprocity gene to kick in before making their sales pitch. Without our instinct for reciprocity, free samples might cease to exist.

Reciprocity works in negotiations, even when one of the parties isn't even aware they are in a negotiation. There is the joke about the little girl who goes to her daddy and asks if she can have a pony. As her daddy explains all the reasons why they can't let her have a pony, the little girl tears up and then asks, "Well, if I can't have a pony, could I have a hamster instead?" The daddy, relieved to have an acceptable alternative, is only too ready to oblige. Later, Daddy overhears the girl talking to her friend. The friend says she didn't even know the girl wanted a pony. The girl replies, "I don't want a pony. But I knew Daddy would say yes to a hamster if he had to say no to a pony first."

This same tactic works very effectively in financial bargaining. People who stake out an extreme first position and then move toward the middle ground wind up with a more favorable outcome than people who stake a more reasonable position and then don't budge. Not only does the person who stakes out a more extreme position come away with a better price, the other party feels better about the outcome, even when they end up paying more as a result of the initially high price.

Reciprocity is part of more intimate relationships, too. Any relationship that has the potential to become more than a mere acquaintance is very sensitive to balance in the early stages. These relationships grow through a balance of give and take, such as gifts, favors, attention, and self-disclosure. Giving too much too early can make you seem needy or potentially exploiting. Giving too little can make you seem cold or selfish.

Reciprocity is a form of mimicking, and mimicking has been proven to make two people feel closer. We like people who mimic us, and we mimic people we like. If a relationship is struggling to move forward or if it has hit a rough spot, reciprocity can help the parties with the mimicking process.

In this world, we have *social norms* and *market norms*. Social norms involve the interactions between humans. They are about helping each other and getting along. They are the glue that holds a society together. They are biological. Market norms involve a bottom line. They are transaction-based. They can be precisely measured. They are mechanical.

We are all familiar with the old saying, "It's a pleasure doing business with you." Conducting business with people should be a pleasurable experience, but there should be clear boundaries where social norms rule and where market norms rule. In any business situation, there is a potential clash of social norms and market norms, and any attempt to mix the two can lead to real problems.

The first thing to realize is that when social norms collide with market norms, social norms lose. This collision almost always occurs when market norms invade the world of social norms. Many budding romantic relationships have come to a screeching halt because, at some point, the guy brought up how much he had spent on dates and that he wasn't getting anything in return. That one comment shifted the relationship from social norms to market norms.

In business relationships, market norms should rule. Every business should treat their customers and their employees with respect. But the business will have neither customers nor employees unless it maintains an acceptable bottom line. In the long term, all employees must be judged on their ability to add value to the business. All customers must be judged on whether they add to or subtract from the bottom line.

If you are an employee, the relationship with your employer should be based first on a fair exchange of labor for money. That said, social norms are one of the best ways to engender employee loyalty. We may stay because we need the paycheck, but we want to stay when we feel appreciated, which is a large purpose of social norms.

In social relationships, social norms should rule. When you are invited to a friend's house for dinner, you bring a nice bottle of wine as a gift; you don't offer to "pay the tab" at the end of the evening. When your neighbor asks to borrow your chain saw, you lend it with the expectation he will return the favor in the future (reciprocity); you don't charge him rent.

Social norms should always prevail when a higher calling is involved. If people want to do something for altruistic reasons, you will offend them and prompt them to withdraw support if you bring money into the equation. The good feeling we get when we do something to help others is priceless, so the worst thing one can do is attempt to put a price on it.

One of the best examples of social norms, market norms, and reciprocity is in *The Godfather*. The opening scene has Bonasera, the undertaker, asking Don

Corleone to kill the men who violated his daughter. The Don replies, "What have I done to make you treat me so disrespectfully? You don't ask this favor out of friendship. Instead you come to my house on the day of my daughter's wedding and ask me to do murder for money." Don Corleone refuses to let market norms trump social norms. He also triggers Bonasera's reciprocity gene when he says, "Someday, and that day may never come, I will call on you to do a service for me."

If you introduce market norms where social norms prevail, market norms will almost always win. But know that social norms may never return and that they never forget, either.

When someone makes a mistake with market norms, the typical result is a loss of business, but nothing more. People who are consistently bad with market norms may end up going out of business, but they probably won't become social pariahs.

Making mistakes with social norms can be far more costly. Our social network, our relationship support system, is undergirded by social norms. When we are clumsy with social norms or when we attempt to replace social norms with market norms, we risk knocking that entire support system out from under us.

Social media has become the most importance place for a business to be if they intend to stay in business. While it may be called social media, it is actually driven by market norms.

While keeping in touch with others' activities is a major driver of social media, the real reason for the popularity of social media is the almost endless opportunities for self-promotion.

BECOMING WHEALTHY

Over time, your social media postings paint a picture of you to others. These postings offer the opportunity for many people to get to know you better. Whether or not that's a good thing depends on what you're posting.

One of the more troubling trends with social media involves generations Y and Z, young people who use social media in greater proportion for their socializing than older people. They may be more adept at communicating in a digital world, but for those relationships to have any real-world value, they must eventually take place in the real world, which means face-to-face. While social media may enable people, especially younger ones, to speak up in situations where they might remain silent in person, the reliance on social media also seems to be hampering the ability to write and speak effectively in more traditional settings.

A sustained presence on social media can have the effect of living in a glass house. Every time you post something, you will be scrutinized by about 150 of your "friends." (The average number of Facebook friends closely coincides with the maximum number in our "village.") The necessity to self-edit can make it harder to be yourself, even when you are in one-on-one situations. You can never be sure what *they* might post about you if you bare your soul to them.

Renowned psychologist Daniel Kahneman contends that one of the best ways to improve our experience is to switch from passive leisure, such as TV watching, to more active forms of leisure, including socializing and exercise. He cites surveys conducted in 150 countries about people's emotions and their causes. He sums up the results of the studies as follows:

BECOMING WHEALTHY

*"The gigantic samples allow extremely fine analyses, which have confirmed the importance of situational factors, physical health, and social contact in experienced well-being. Not surprisingly, a headache will make a person miserable, and the second best indicator of the feelings of a day is whether a person did or did not have contacts with friends or relatives. It is only a slight exaggeration to say that **happiness is the experience of spending time with people you love and who love you.**"* (emphasis mine)

What Kahneman's and others' research has shown is that one of the best ways to achieve emotional and physical health is to reduce passive solitary activities like watching TV alone, and replace those activities with physical activities you can share with others, especially if those others are people who are important to you.

Throughout history, man was strongly discouraged to be self-sufficient, autonomous. This concept seems strange to Americans, who have prided themselves on their "rugged individualism. It's not a coincidence that the nation with the strongest love of autonomy also has the greatest material wealth.

Before money and without money, the kind of autonomy Americans simultaneously cherish and take for granted could not exist. Without money, market norms would cease to exist, and all you would be left with are social norms. When you have money, and it doesn't take a lot of it, you can afford to treat others badly. As long as you can afford to pay for the essentials in life, you don't have to worry that alienating large segments of the population will cause you any real deprivations.

BECOMING WHEALTHY

As necessary as money is in our lives, it isn't as necessary as relationships. And while money and relationships are not mutually exclusive, we too often choose one and let the other wither. Both have a place in our lives. Money is our primary method of contact with the world that doesn't comprise our personal village of 150. Money is essential. Without money, we would have no mutually beneficial contact with most of humanity.

When it comes to our village of 150, those people in our lives with whom we have relationships, money should not only be secondary; money should avoid any place in the relationship if at all possible. Whenever money comes in contact with something, it puts a price on that thing - that is the role of money. Our most precious relationships are to be prized - not priced.

In the animal kingdom, most interactions are a zero-sum game. One animal gains at the other's expense. When humans revert to their more animalistic instincts, we also think in terms of zero-sum games. In such a frame of mind, every encounter becomes a win-lose situation.

A zero-sum game assumes that resources are not only finite, but that they cannot be increased at all. However, man's ability to create wealth also creates opportunities for all parties to benefit. The ability to create wealth, combined with the ability to cooperate, also creates the possibility of win-win situations. However, in order for win-win relationships to form and to endure, the parties involved all have to find a way to cooperate without being exploited.

Tit-for-tat, quid pro quo, reciprocity, whatever you call it, seems ingrained in our human nature. We have an innate desire to trade compliments, insults, favors, and abuses. The Ultimatum game is a game often played in economic experiments in which two players interact to decide how to divide a sum of money that is given to them. The first player proposes how to divide the sum between the two players, and the second player can either accept or reject this proposal. If the second player rejects, neither player receives anything. If the second player accepts, the money is split according to the proposal. The game is played only once so that reciprocation/retaliation is not an issue.

Logic would dictate that the second player should always accept the offer. After all, to reject the offer means to receive no money at all. However, the issues of greed, fairness, and reprisal often overcome logic. If the offer by the first player is deemed insufficient by the second, the second player will reject the offer, if only to keep the first player from receiving an "unfair" reward.

Our tendency is to create a lose-lose situation if the only alternative is to allow a win-lose situation where we are the loser. If we feel that the winner in such a situation had an unfair advantage, we are quite willing to hurt ourselves if our actions will hurt the other person more. Such is the perspective of the suicide bomber.

In financial dealings, it is expected that people will act in their own self-interest, which includes working hard for the best deal. If you think that all financial dealings are a zero-sum game, where any gain by the other party must come at your expense, you will see every business deal as a win-lose situation. That perspective will make you confrontational, not cooperative, but long-term financial success is based on a win-win strategy, by cooperating so that all parties benefit from the transaction.

Those who succeed in business understand that for a business to survive for decades, to generate profits for decades, and to have a serious market value when it's time to sell it, that business must be run from the concept that every deal should be a win-win for the buyer and the seller. This philosophy is based on cooperation, not confrontation, or even competition. It is necessary for the business to win in order to stay in business. It is necessary for the customer to win to enable the customer to be a repeat customer and to refer others to the business.

Win-win enables each party to feel they win without having to consider how the other party feels. That feeling is not contingent on the other party's feeling like a loser in the deal. The other party's happiness adds to your happiness; it does not take away from it.

With a win-lose strategy, a win is defined less by what deal you actually got than by how unhappy the other party is about the deal. If the other party acts like a winner in the deal, it can make you feel like something was left on the table.

The only time anyone deals with a person who takes a win-lose mindset is when there are no other options. A win-lose attitude is a weakness that competitors will eventually exploit. People naturally want to work with someone who is cooperative, not confrontational, which is why a win-lose mentality makes long-term success almost impossible.

Attachment theory describes the long-term relationships between humans. One of its tenets is that an infant needs to develop a relationship with a primary caregiver (typically the mother) for mental, social, and emotional development to occur.

Attachment theory posits that two basic goals guide a child's behavior: safety and exploration. A child who stays safe will survive, but a child who explores and plays will develop the skills and intelligence needed to function in adult society. When the child feels safe, the child plays and explores. However, when the child perceives a drop in the safety level, such as when a parent is no longer visible, the child stops playing and safety needs become paramount.

In the 1970's, researchers Ellen Berscheid and Elaine Walster proposed the distinction between *passionate love* and *companionate love*. They describe passionate love as a "wildly emotional state in which tender and sexual feelings, elation and pain, anxiety and relief, altruism and jealousy coexist in a confusion of feelings." In contrast, they describe companionate love as "the affection we feel for those with whom our lives are deeply intertwined." In passionate love, you look deeply into each other's eyes. In companionate love, you look deeply in the same direction.

Passionate love is like being high on a drug and, like a drug high, eventually there is a coming down to normal. Passionate love has high intensity but short duration. Companionate love has far lower intensity, but it not only has a far longer duration, it typically grows stronger over time.

In studies comparing couples who chose their own spouses with couples in arranged marriages, passionate love was the main driver for those who chose their own spouses. In contrast, most people who were in arranged marriages barely knew their spouses before taking vows. Their love developed as companionate love, often with a dose of passionate love as a bonus. Because those who arranged the marriages focused on companionate love instead of passionate love, the arranged marriages had a much higher success rate than those freely created out of passionate love.

BECOMING WHEALTHY

Passionate love does not change into companionate love because they are two separate processes with two very different time courses. When we see a couple that has been married for fifty years, we admire their ability to create and sustain a companionate love over several decades. We are not admiring any ability to remain hot for each other over that period of time because, frankly, that's beyond human capabilities.

Our most enduring and most important relationships are those we have with members of our family. Despite disagreements, conflicts, ego clashes, and all the rest, when we most need someone to break our fall or lift us up, we tend to look first to a family member.

There is one problem with our dependence on family relationships - the size of the average family is shrinking around the world. Each generation is seeing a smaller support system of aunts, uncles, cousins, and siblings. Some forty percent of children in the U.S. also live in single-parent homes. In addition, families are now spread out all over the country. Only a couple of generations ago, it was not unusual to have three generations under one roof. Now it is becoming unusual to find three generations within one *state*.

As families have become more dispersed, neighborhoods have become less homogeneous, too. When neighborhoods were comprised largely of one or two ethnic groups, there was a greater tendency to see those neighbors as an extended family because there was a common background and a common language. The parents in the neighborhood acted as surrogate parents for all the children in the neighborhood, and the children knew that defying one of your friend's parents was the same as defying your own.

The loss of deeper relationships based on family, faith, and community cannot be offset by the shallow relationships of casual acquaintance, and they certainly cannot be replaced by the disembodied contact of social media. We grow as human beings in proportion to the breadth and the depth of our relationships, in the same way that a tree grows in proportion to the depth and breadth of its root system.

Shallow roots, even those that are spread far, cannot provide water and nourishment when there is drought. Those shallow roots also can't hold the tree in place when there is severe weather. Our shallow relationships cannot be counted on to provide sustenance or keep us grounded when life really starts coming down hard on us. Those shallow relationships are the proverbial fair-weather friends.

It takes greater effort to develop a few deep relationships than it does to generate several shallow ones, just as it takes more effort for a tree to put down deep roots than it does to spread many shallow ones. But it's the deep relationships that will save you when things are at their worst. A few deep relationships are preferable to many shallow ones. Quality is preferable to quantity.

When you lack meaningful relationships in your life, the result is isolation and loneliness. Loneliness has been proven to have serious negative effects on a person's well-being, including but not limited to serious damage to one's physical health and financial stability.

In a study of 45,000 people ages 45 and up who had heart disease or were at high risk for developing the condition, those who lived alone were more likely to die from heart attacks, strokes, or other complications than people living with family, friends, or in some other communal arrangement. The risk was highest in middle-aged people. Among those 45 to 65 years of age, solo living increased the risk of heart problems and early death by 24%, compared to only 12% among those ages 66 to 80, and a negligible increase among those over 80.

The six-year study found that men and women were 45% more likely to die during the study if they reported feeling lonely, isolated, or left out. They were also 59% more likely to have difficulty with everyday tasks, which is an important measure of health in older people.

Some experts view persistent loneliness as a form of stress, which is linked with inflammation and other processes that damage blood vessels. In lonely people who see the world as a threatening place, loneliness raises levels of the circulating stress hormone cortisol and raises blood pressure.

The cycle created by loneliness can be a downward spiral. Lonely people rate their own social interactions more negatively and form worse impressions of people they meet. Lonely people are more likely to overreact to negative behaviors in other people, causing them to fall into a deeper state of loneliness.

Evolution may play a part in the physical damage caused by loneliness. Loneliness not only makes people feel unhappy - it makes them unsafe, mentally and physically. This powerful evolutionary force bound together prehistoric people, enabling them to hunt, raise their young, and continue on as a species. The distress people feel when they drift toward the edges of society can serve as a warning - like physical pain - that it's time to reengage or face danger.

Loneliness is also a matter of perception - it is the discrepancy between your actual and your desired level of contact. Someone can be alone a good deal of the time and not feel lonely, if their level of social contact meets his/her desires for such. It's also possible to feel deep loneliness even when there are people around every minute of the day.

Loneliness takes a toll on financial health, too. We know that loneliness is a perceived shortage of quality relationships. We also know that loneliness makes it harder to develop quality relationships because the lonely person may be over-defensive when attempting to establish a new relationship. One of the keys to sustained financial success is the ability to develop and maintain relationships with a variety of people. Whether you are a business owner or work in a large organization, your success will be determined in large part by how well you relate with others. The condition of loneliness greatly impairs the ability to form the kinds of relationships that lead to sustained prosperity.

Financial problems can also trigger a downward spiral of loneliness and further financial problems. Serious financial problems can cause disruptions in living arrangements and relationships. Financial setbacks may necessitate a move to another town or to the poor side of town. The strength of many of our relationships gets tested during times of financial hardship. The most important relationship, that of husband and wife, can be broken by sustained financial stress. Financial stress can create loneliness, and loneliness can create financial stress. It often isn't easy to tell cause from effect. Whichever one came first, one thing is certain - loneliness and poverty know each other well.

There is one well-documented remedy for those who suffer from any combination of health issues, financial problems, and a shortage of relationships - a relationship with a higher power.

BECOMING WHEALTHY

Studies dating back over two centuries demonstrate that people who have a relationship with a higher power, however they perceive that higher power, are better able to handle the ups and downs of life, including the disappointments that often come with interpersonal relationships. When all the human relationships seem to fail, knowing that your relationship with the Almighty will never fail has been enough to sustain billions of people over thousands of years.

Many people may view prayer as a futile attempt to get God to grant our wishes. The essence of prayer, though, is not petition; it's conversation. Prayer is, or should be, your chance to talk to God about everything that is going on in your life. People who maintain a relationship with a higher power are also better at maintaining relationships with us lower powers, in part because they maintain reasonable expectations from us humans.

BECOMING WHEALTHY

Becoming UNSTOPPABLE

IF by Rudyard Kipling

If you can keep your head when all about you
Are losing theirs and blaming it on you;
If you can trust yourself when all men doubt you,
But make allowance for their doubting too;
If you can wait and not be tired by waiting,
Or, being lied about, don't deal in lies,
Or being hated don't give way to hating,
And yet don't look too good, nor talk too wise;

If you can dream - and not make dreams your master;
If you can think - and not make thoughts your aim;
If you can meet with Triumph and Disaster
And treat those two impostors just the same;
If you can bear to hear the truth you've spoken
Twisted by knaves to make a trap for fools,
Or watch the things you gave your life to, broken,
And stoop and build them up with worn-out tools;

If you can make one heap of all your winnings
And risk it on one turn of pitch-and-toss,
And lose, and start again at your beginnings,
And never breathe a word about your loss;
If you can force your heart and nerve and sinew
To serve your turn long after they are gone,
And so hold on when there is nothing in you
Except the Will which says to them: "Hold on!"

If you can talk with crowds and keep your virtue,
Or walk with Kings---nor lose the common touch;

BECOMING WHEALTHY

If neither foes nor loving friends can hurt you;
If all men count with you, but none too much;
If you can fill the unforgiving minute
With sixty seconds' worth of distance run,
Yours is the Earth and everything that's in it,
And - which is more - you'll be a Man, my son!

Could you pass the "Marshmallow Test?"

In the spring of 1968, Walter Mischel, a psychology professor at Stanford University, conducted an experiment with four-year-olds. Each child was given a marshmallow. They were told that they could eat it any time they wanted, but if they would wait approximately fifteen minutes before eating it, they would be given a second marshmallow. Approximately a third of the children waited; the others could not resist that long.

At the time of the marshmallow experiment, it was assumed that the ability of the child to delay eating the marshmallow was inversely proportionate to how strongly the child craved the marshmallow. But it was soon obvious that *all* the children craved the marshmallow to roughly the same degree.

The children who were able to delay gratification did so largely by diverting their attention away from the marshmallow. They would cover their eyes, play hide-and-seek, sing songs, anything to take their mind off the marshmallow.

These children were demonstrating *metacognition*, which can be defined as thinking about thinking, or knowing about knowing. Maintaining motivation to see a task through to completion is a metacognitive skill, which is what these children were doing by taking their minds off the marshmallows. Metacognition can be instinctive, but can be learned as well. By simply being told to think of the marshmallow as just a picture of a marshmallow, the children could increase their delay period from less than one minute to over fifteen minutes.

The marshmallow experiment is a powerfully predictive test. As Mischel explains it, "If you can deal with hot emotions, then you can study for the SAT instead of watching television, and you can save more money for retirement. It's not just about marshmallows."

Psychology professor Angela Lee Duckworth has conducted similar experiments with eighth-graders. They were given the choice of a dollar right away or two dollars the following week. Duckworth found that the ability to delay gratification was a far better predictor of academic performance than IQ. In her own words, "Intelligence is really important, but it's still not as important as self-control." These findings confirm that talent means nothing without persistence and discipline.

The researchers followed the development of each child in the marshmallow experiment through adolescence. They found that those children who had demonstrated the ability to wait in the marshmallow experiment were better adjusted and more dependable, based on surveys of the children's parents and teachers. Even more significant perhaps, the students who could delay gratification scored an average of 210 points higher on the SAT's than their less disciplined peers.

In this chapter, we will use two terms frequently - willpower and self-control. While they have similarities, they are also different. Self-control is more habit than activity. Self-control is what is exerted on a daily basis, often without you being fully aware that you are exerting it. Willpower is typically summoned during moments of crisis or great temptation. As our self-control develops, we actually increase our ability to summon willpower as needed, while also needing it less frequently. People with high self-control are confirmed as having less stress in their lives. Their focus is on avoiding crises, rather than merely surviving them.

Self-control and willpower can be compared to two measurements of your car engine's output - horsepower and torque. Self-control is like horsepower; willpower is like torque.

Horsepower measures the rate at which work is done. The formula is a calculation of how much weight gets moved how far in how much time. When we think of high horsepower, we think of fast cars like Corvettes and Ferraris.

Torque is a measurement of twisting or turning force. If you've ever used a wrench to loosen a nut or bolt, you were exerting torque. When we think of high torque in an engine, we think of big trucks that have to keep the engine turning even when they are hauling a load of logs up a steep grade.

You need a combination of self-control and willpower, just like an engine needs a combination of horsepower and torque. Self-control alone is like horsepower alone - you can zoom along at a high speed but you can't carry the logs up the hill when you need to. Willpower alone is like torque alone. You may be exerting a huge effort, but you can't sustain it for long and you may still not make any progress.

You have probably tried loosening a nut that wouldn't budge, no matter how much torque you exerted. You may have also exerted a great deal of willpower only to fail at what you were trying to achieve or avoid. Self-control tends to have benefits that reflect the effort expended, which is much less the case with willpower. Self-control is a good habit to develop simply because it provides a better return on investment than does willpower alone.

The marshmallow experiment was a study of delayed gratification. Delaying gratification is just one aspect of self-control, but it may be the most important one. When you're a creature with an eighty year lifespan, many of the circumstances of your life are the result of decisions you have made in the past. Many of those decisions involved saying no to something desirable at that moment in order to get something even more desirable in the future.

There are two essential personal traits that psychologists say are essential to "positive outcomes," or what we call success. The two traits are intelligence and self-control. While we have spent trillions of dollars trying to increase the overall intelligence of the population, very little attention and even less money has been spent on trying to increase the average person's self-control.

Think about the big problems we face, as individuals and as a society. Now think about how many of those problems - excess debt, excess weight, drug abuse, violence, underachievement in school and at work, to name a few - have at their root cause, a fundamental lack of self-control.

We devote a lot of time, effort, and money to developing our muscles. Willpower is like a mental muscle; it can become fatigued with overuse. It can also become stronger over time through regular exercise. Exercising willpower can also do more to improve our quality of life than exercising our muscles can.

The problems we create through insufficient willpower do not mean that people aren't exercising willpower. Researchers estimate that the average American spends a good four hours a day resisting temptations like food, sleep, or sex. In addition to these age-old temptations, we have modern ones like video games, e-mail, Facebook, and cable TV. There are so many more temptations today than in the past that we need to upgrade our self-control skills just to survive, much less to succeed.

Researchers comparing college students' grades with over thirty personality traits have discovered that self-control is the only trait that predicts college grades better than chance, and it is a far better predictor than IQ or SAT scores. On the job, managers who exhibit self-control are rated more highly by both peers and subordinates. Children with poor self-control end up sicker, poorer, and are far more likely to eventually end up in prison.

The human brain composes 2% of our body, but uses 20% of the body's energy. Our brain is very large as a percentage of our body, compared to other animals. One reason for this discrepancy is our large frontal lobe, which is the part of the brain that is vital for creating and maintaining complex social networks.

Our complex social networks create a greater need for self-control because the more interactions you have with others in your species, the more possibilities there are to do something that will cause harm to you or others. Because human survival was and is predicated on our ability to interact (it's our best and pretty much our only survival skill), anything that jeopardizes our ability to interact properly with others, like a lack of self-control, is potentially fatal.

Self-control is the key to co-existing with other people. It is also the key to accomplishing any task that requires real and sustained effort. Self-control is an ongoing habit that lets you relax. The habit of self-control reduces stress and lets you conserve willpower for those important challenges.

Self-control is like the habit of exercise. Once you have it, you can better handle a sudden demand on your muscles, like saving someone from drowning. Willpower is like that sudden demand to physically act beyond the norm. You can handle it because you were in shape, though you do still get fatigued.

Because willpower is an exhaustible resource like muscle strength, there is only so much to go around at any time. Marital problems increase when one of the partners is suffering stress at work. Stress at work takes a lot of willpower to overcome, and by the time the person gets home, the willpower supply is depleted and there is none left to handle whatever stress might be waiting at home.

Marathons are 26.2 miles long. There is a saying in marathon running - at 20 miles you're halfway there. At 20 miles your body has also used up all its conventional energy sources. At some point after mile 20, the human body wants to, begs to quit, and willpower is the only thing that gets a runner to the finish line.

The diminished capacity to regulate one's thoughts, feelings, and actions is known as *ego depletion*. Energy is consumed by exerting willpower or making decisions, and once the energy level is sufficiently drained, self-control can ebb quickly. Signs of ego depletion include stronger emotional reactions, both positive and negative. Sensitivity to pain increases. Desires become stronger. Ego depletion is characterized, not by specific symptoms, but by an increase in the intensity of feelings. This increased sensitivity can lead to negative behaviors, from increased alcohol consumption to aggressive encounters to reckless sexual behavior.

Ego depletion can be harmful in two ways: desires increase at the same time willpower is depleted. Pity the drug addict going through withdrawal. The amount of willpower required to break an addiction is staggering. That huge drain of energy causes ego depletion and increases the craving for the drug at the same time the addict is stopping use of the drug.

Stress depletes willpower, too. During final exam periods, college students typically eat more, drink more, have more frequent sex, and sleep less. If the students have been procrastinating all semester, the stress is greater as they rush to complete term papers while cramming a semester's worth of reading into two weeks.

You have a finite supply of willpower, and it is not broken into compartments. If you use a lot of willpower to quit smoking, you are not going to have much left to also start exercising. If you expend a lot of energy exercising one afternoon, it doesn't surprise you when you're too tired to go out dancing that evening. You don't have separate tanks for exercise energy and dancing energy. You don't have separate tanks for non-smoking willpower and exercise willpower, either.

Chronic pain leads to a depletion of willpower. It takes a lot of energy to ignore or overcome constant pain. Chronic pain is physically and psychologically exhausting. One reason people with chronic pain can be so grouchy is they have no willpower to resist saying something when something or someone bothers them.

Because willpower is a renewable but finite, resource, taking on numerous challenges that simultaneously require willpower is a recipe for failure. The reason most New Year's resolutions fail often isn't a lack of total willpower in the individual; the willpower is being allocated to too many tasks at once. It's like water pressure in your house - flush the toilet and you suddenly lose pressure in the shower. It's better to focus on one challenge, to give it all you've got, and then to move on to the next one when you've reached your goal. That feeling of accomplishment can also serve as motivation on the next challenge.

Even if you only take on one resolution, if your willpower muscles are weak and flabby, you may find yourself failing sooner than you ever expected. If you want to quit smoking, lose weight, and exercise regularly, trying to do all three at once won't work. Tackling the most difficult one first also won't work if you've never demonstrated much willpower up to now.

The better course is to first tackle the challenge you have the most confidence of completing. The willpower muscles you build in meeting that challenge will serve you in meeting bigger challenges later.

Looked at another way, you wouldn't start exercising with 50 lb. weights and then move to 40 lb. and then 30 lb. weights. You start with the lighter weight, acclimate to it, then graduate to the bigger challenge of greater weight.

According to a 2007 study in the *New England Journal of Medicine,* 40% of all deaths can be attributed to what behavioral researchers call poor self-regulation, the technical term for self-control. This poor self-regulation, or lack of willpower or self-control, is the reason 45 million Americans still smoke, two-thirds of us are overweight, and 600,000 die from cardiovascular disease every year.

To regulate means to guide toward a specific goal. One of the reasons for setting clear goals is that self-regulation, or self-control, requires goals in order to work. No goals, no self-control; no self-control, your life is a mess.

Most of us have too many goals, rather than too few. One of the reasons we have multiple goals is because we have multiple messes in our lives. We can really only handle one mess at a time, though. Working on one goal, cleaning up one mess at a time, offers a good chance of success. Trying to tackle more, even just two at once, practically guarantees you won't reach any goals.

There is a strong link between decision-making and willpower, and the two affect each other. Decision-making saps willpower, and once willpower is sapped, it is more difficult to make decisions - at least good ones.

Decision-making is, at its core, the process of making choices. Everyone loves to have choices - Heinz has 57 varieties; Baskin-Robbins has 31 flavors. Having a wider variety of choices is desirable - in theory. In reality, more choices require more effort to make a decision. More choices also mean foregoing more options which, when our willpower is already depleted from having to decide, is even harder to do.

If you have a 401(k) or similar retirement plan at work, you also have an array of investment options. If you had ten to fifteen mutual funds from which to choose, you could probably digest the material and pick a combination of funds that would be appropriate to your needs and goals. However, if you were given fifty to sixty mutual fund choices, your task would become much more difficult.

Studies have shown that employees who have a larger array of investment options in their retirement plans are more likely to go with the default option which, in most cases, is too conservative to meet an employee's goals. Most of us don't have the willpower needed to make an informed decision in this case. As a result, many people will have to work longer or suffer a diminished standard of living in retirement.

We have all seen advertising that uses attractive women to sell items that seem to have no relationship to attractive women or sex. Studies have shown that men seek more immediate rewards when stimulated by the presence of an attractive woman, even if it's just a picture of a woman.

The sight of an attractive woman stimulates the brain's nucleus accumbens, a primitive part of the brain which is activated by rewards, like cash and candy and hot babes. If an attractive woman is promoting a product, a man is more likely to splurge on that product. Advertisers have known for decades that the Achilles Heel of most men's willpower is a good-looking woman.

Wealth is created with only two ingredients - work and delayed gratification. Work creates money, but only delayed gratification turns it into wealth. The main ingredient in delayed gratification is self-control. Even if the goal isn't wealth, delayed gratification is the only thing standing between us and dire poverty in our senior years. Delayed gratification is more than a wealth-building skill; it's a survival skill.

Health also requires self-control in two distinct areas. One area is the same delayed gratification that is used to build wealth. We don't always have to say "no" to anything that is enjoyable and unhealthy, but we at least need the ability to say "not now" more often than most of us do.

Perhaps more than any other single factor, the keys to becoming whealthy lie in:
a) your ability to say "not now" when you are tempted by things that bring short-term pleasure but long-term pain;
b) your ability to avoid saying "not now" when you are tempted not to do things that bring short-term pain but long-term gain.

It's hard to develop and maintain self-control if you aren't very diligent about monitoring your behavior. Self-control requires self-awareness, and self-awareness is a product of monitoring one's own behavior.

A major aspect of self-awareness is the process of comparing ourselves to some standard. That standard might be internally generated, but we often set standards based on the behaviors of others. A classic example of the latter is when otherwise law-abiding individuals degenerate into a mob because mob behavior suddenly becomes the standard.

Self-control requires self-awareness. We become self-aware through comparisons with others. We also have our own conscience which reminds us that, just because everyone else is doing something, that doesn't make it acceptable for us to do it, too. In an experiment where people were instructed to give shocks to another person, those who were seated in front of a mirror were less likely to do so. The ability to see themselves in the mirror also made them more likely to complete tasks and less likely to change their opinion when pressured by others.

Social media offers many opportunities to say something that will come back to haunt you. Self-control is certainly a necessity when using social media, unless you don't care how your words affect you or others, especially those closest to you.

Social media and other methods of making our private information public can be useful from the standpoint of monitoring. People are often more concerned about how others perceive them than they are about how they perceive themselves. When we take it upon ourselves to publicize aspects of our lives, we are also inviting others to share in the job of monitoring us. When we're not sure if we're doing the right thing or whether we'll have the willpower to do the right thing, by going public we can outsource some of that responsibility to others.

Studies have shown that exercising self-control in one area leads to improvements in other areas, even when a conscious effort isn't made to improve those other areas. Smokers who begin to exercise regularly discover they're smoking less, even though they haven't made a conscious effort to reduce their smoking. People who begin a regular savings plan find themselves unconsciously becoming more self-controlled and savvy in their spending.

As you practice self-control, you increase your supply of willpower. That extra willpower is available to use in other areas that need help, and you may find yourself using willpower in those areas almost by accident. Also, as you practice self-control in one area, your actions become habits, and we know that habits require less thought and less willpower than other activities. The end result is you increase your supply of willpower at the same time that you require less willpower in the area on which you are focusing. This dual benefit is why you can become whealthy. You can improve in more than one area simultaneously by using less of a resource that is also increasing in supply.

Contrary to what you might first think, a long-term focus does more to improve self-control than a short-term focus does. Thinking broad and abstract, instead of narrow and concrete, and thinking in terms of why, rather than how, helps us to see the bigger picture.

Which do you think comes first with high school students - high self-esteem or high grades? If you listen to the advocates of the self-esteem movement, high self-esteem leads to high grades. While it is true that children with high self-esteem tend to have higher grades, the self-esteem advocates have the order in reverse.

Students' grades in tenth grade have accurately predicted those students' self-esteem in twelfth grade; students' self-esteem in tenth grade did not at all predict their grades in twelfth grade. These findings merely confirm what most people know from common sense: self-esteem is the product of accomplishment; accomplishment is the product of sacrifice, and sacrifice is possible only through self-control. How else can you explain students' self-esteem rising while their scholastic performance has declined?

High self-esteem without a foundation of accomplishment leads to narcissism. When young people enter the adult world and are informed that they are not as smart, beautiful, witty, or charismatic as they think they are, it's a real comedown. Making the situation worse is many young people's lack of training on building self-control to create achievements that generate self-esteem. Too many young people will have to learn at twenty-nine what they should have learned at nine.

BECOMING WHEALTHY

Since it was first published in 1989, Steven Covey's book *The 7 Habits of Highly Effective People* has sold more than 25 million copies worldwide. It ranks in the top ten best-selling non-fiction books of all time. Habit 2 is titled "Begin with the End in Mind." The author explains:

"To begin with the end in mind means to start with a clear understanding of your destination. It means to know where you're going so that you better understand where you are now and so that the steps you take are always in the right direction... we may be very busy, we may be very efficient, but we will also be truly <u>effective</u> only when we begin with the end in mind."

Inspiration and motivation are your sails; goals are your rudder.

Before you can set goals, you must first determine what your mission is. When you think of your mission, you should think in terms of a personal philosophy and set of values that don't change. Goals can and should change as needed.

Developing your own mission statement is important because it puts the horse before the cart. The goals you set will develop from the mission statement. The goals you set will have a tremendous effect on both your success and your happiness. If you set goals that are not in alignment with who you are and what you believe in, you may be successful in achieving them, but you will never achieve happiness.

Once you have your inspiration, your motivation, and your mission statement, the next step is to set some goals to help you actually achieve what you now know you want to achieve.

Almost all of the goals someone would set in the quest to become whealthy would be termed *behavioral* goals. Since almost all of the impediments to becoming whealthy are caused by personal behavior, it makes sense to work on changing behaviors first.

Behaviors are the causes; everything that you are looking to change are the effects. You don't change the effects by attempting to change the effects; you change the effects by changing the causes.

In truth, we can almost never directly control outcomes. Trying to directly control an outcome very often requires breaking the rules. If you understand and separate in your mind causes and effects, you will be able to spend your time and energy on what you can actually control, which are inputs, not outcomes.

The causes and effects that lead to becoming whealthy are not that complicated. If you eat at a fast food restaurant five times a week and if you have a weight problem, then the two are very likely a cause-effect relationship. If you increase your contributions to your 401(k) plan, then you are very likely to cause the effect of having more money at retirement.

In recent years, American business has embraced the concept of SMART goals. The acronym stands for **S**pecific, **M**easurable, **A**chievable, **R**ealistic, and **T**ime-targeted. The concept of SMART goals contends that goals that are difficult to achieve and specific tend to increase performance more than goals that are not.

Setting SMART goals affects outcomes in four ways:
- **Choice**: goals narrow attention and direct efforts to goal-relevant activities and away from counter-productive or irrelevant activities.

- **Effort**: goals can lead to more effort, especially because a goal almost always exceeds the current level of performance.
- **Persistence**: Someone becomes more prone to work through the inevitable setbacks if pursuing a goal.
- **Cognition**: Goals can lead individuals to develop and change their behavior in the long run, even after goals are met.

Because SMART goals are specific, they avoid some of the biggest flaws in goal-setting - irrelevance and ambiguity. SMART goals can be very effective, but only if the goals themselves are worthwhile. Before goals, especially SMART goals, are created and implemented, everyone who is expected to meet those goals needs to believe that what they are working toward is worth the effort to get there. SMART goals presume a commitment; they don't create it.

The need to buy into a goal before attempting to achieve it is the reason for inspiration and motivation first. If you are setting goals only for yourself, becoming inspired and motivated can be fairly easy. If you have to inspire and motivate others, that's defined as Leadership, which is in essence inspiring and motivating others to do what they would not do on their own. For our purposes, we will limit our discussion to personal goal-setting. If you are able to achieve your own goals, that's enough for now.

A goal of losing twenty pounds in six months is Specific, Measurable, Achievable, Realistic, and Time-targeted (SMART). However, before a goal like this has any chance of success, a behavioral goal needs to go in front of it. The behavioral goal might be to reduce the weekly visits to fast food restaurants from five to one and to eat something light at home for those four meals.

The behavioral goal makes the SMART goal possible, but the SMART goal is the motivator to achieve the behavioral goal.

Financial goals are difficult to achieve, more difficult to achieve than health goals. Financial goals can tend to be rather sterile, too. If your financial goal is to save $10,000 in one year, that may be a SMART goal, but financial goals tend to involve more short-term pain for long-term gain than other goals.

When you consider what you have to give up over the next year to save $10,000, it's a challenge. However, if you put the financial goal into a different perspective, the trade-offs become worth it.

The impetus to save $10,000 may come from an embarrassing episode when you had to borrow money from in-laws to get the car repaired. The thought of having to listen to another lecture on financial responsibility, delayed gratification, etc. from your in-laws is the real driving force behind your savings goal. It's helpful to remind yourself of that embarrassment when the temptation to spend instead of save gets too strong.

Restrictive goals are goals that leave no wiggle room, no ambiguity, and no room for interpretation. They are black and white. If you are trying to lose weight, a restrictive goal might be "No ice cream." You set that goal because ice cream is your Achilles Heel. You realize that as long as ice cream is allowed to be part of your diet, your chances of losing weight are slim (pun intended).

Restrictive goals can be effective if they are not permanent. Restrictive goals are also not inspiring. In order to be effective, restrictive goals need to be married to long-term goals with emotional resonance.

BECOMING WHEALTHY

We've all heard the Chinese saying: a journey of a thousand miles begins with a single step. There are two purposes behind that saying. The first purpose is to remind us that the first step is the most difficult one to make; the second is to remind us that big goals are accomplished through several of small accomplishments.

Most of us want to save more and weigh less. When we think of setting goals in these areas, we think of ourselves as starting from scratch, which can be discouraging.

Let's assume you have some money saved or that you have successfully lost weight in the past. You can use those as points in your favor. You aren't starting to save; you are moving further up the savings ladder. You aren't starting to lose weight; you are re-engaging the momentum you had before.

Most of the goals we set for ourselves are too audacious, or at least too audaciously stated. If you stated a goal of walking a thousand miles, it sounds impressive, but it also sounds intimidating to the point that the first step might never get taken. On the other hand, setting a goal of walking two miles a day is not intimidating, and in less than seventeen months you can cover a thousand miles.

Even if you could knock out a big goal in one grand gesture, it might not be the best approach to take. When it comes to knocking out a goal, it's better to act like a piranha than a python. A python eats a meal at one time that can last for months. Of course, the python is actually immobile for some time after consuming an animal big enough to satisfy its hunger. Piranha take many small bites instead of consuming a victim whole. The python's method is boom and bust; the piranha's method is steady as she goes.

BECOMING WHEALTHY

If you've ever decided to start an exercise program like a python, you might have exercised vigorously for two hours the first day. As a result, you were in pain and unable to exercise at all for several days. Had you taken the piranha approach and nibbled a little more exercise each day, you would have avoided the physical and emotional backlash. You would have become fitter each day. And you would have remained motivated by knowing you could do a little more the next time.

When taking on a new challenge, your goal at the outset should be to become better than you are now; your goal should not be to become your best, at least not yet. Expecting to go from scratch to the best you can be almost guarantees failure in achieving the goal, with a crushed spirit as collateral damage.

It is not only acceptable, but expected that you will ramp up your goals as you achieve them. You don't go from saving nothing to saving $100 a week. You start by saving $10 and increasing the amount over time, as quickly as you are able. You also don't go from doing nothing to doing 100 sit-ups a day. You start by doing 10 and increase the number over time, as quickly as you are able

You may think that setting small goals leads to less success because you aren't pushing yourself, but that isn't the case. Small goals that get accomplished do more to spur us on than do large single goals that always seem to be over the horizon. The positive reinforcement that achieving small goals provides enables us to continue making progress toward larger goals.

Research shows that small goals, known in psychology as proximal goals, have more effect than large goals, known as distal goals. In one study, elementary school students who did poorly in math were broken into two groups. One group was given the distal goal of completing seven thirty-minute math modules by the end of the seventh session. The other group was given the proximal goal of completing one module during each session.

Both groups were functioning at the same math skills level at the beginning. On the final test, the distal goals group solved 45% of the problems; the proximal goals group solved 81%. The only difference in the two groups in this study was in the way the goals were presented. The distal group was thinking like a python; the proximal group was thinking like a piranha. The results speak for themselves.

Dean Karlan is an economics professor at Yale University. Along with colleagues Barry Nalebuff and Ian Ayres, he developed stickK.com. StickK.com offers you the opportunity, through "Commitment Contracts," to show to yourself and others the value you put on achieving your goals.

The four steps involved on stickK.com are:
1. **Select your goal.** Your goal can be anything you want. No guidance is offered on setting appropriate or attainable goals.
2. **Set the stakes.** You have the option of putting money on the line. If you don't succeed in meeting your goal, stickK will send your money to one of three options - a friend, a charity, or an "anti-charity," which is an organization you choose that is against what you stand for. The thought of financially supporting the other side can be a powerful motivator.
3. **Get a referee.** Invite someone trustworthy to be your referee and report to stickK.com your success or failure.

4. **Add friends for support.** Your friends can supply support, peer pressure, or whatever you might need to help you meet your goal.

One of the reasons stickK.com was developed is the knowledge, backed by research, that writing down one's goals significantly increases the success rate in achieving those goals. One study conducted by Dominican University looked at 149 participants who varied widely by age, occupation, and nationality. The overall data showed that those who wrote down their goals had a success rate 50% higher than those who did not write down their goals.

A study done in Scotland in 1992 demonstrated the healing power of written goals. A group of sixty patients who had hip or knee replacement surgery were studied during rehab. Movement is very painful after such surgery, but it is essential to get moving as soon as possible.

Each patient received a booklet with his/her rehab schedule. In the back of the booklet were several additional blank pages with a heading: "My goals for this week are____:" The patients were asked to write down their personal rehab goals for each week, such as when and how far they planned to walk that week.

When the researchers followed up with the patients three months later, they found a profound difference between those who had written down weekly goals and those who hadn't. The patients who had written goals had begun walking nearly twice as fast as the ones who hadn't. They became mobile almost three times faster.

Almost everyone responds better to positive reinforcement than to the negative kind. For that reason, goals are more effective when stated in positive terms rather than negative ones. A goal that is stated in terms of what someone is moving toward, rather than what they hope to leave behind, will be more effective. For example, it's preferable to state a goal of becoming sober, as opposed to stating it as stopping drinking.

Goals need to be quantifiable, which means that, whenever possible, a date and an amount of some kind should be part of a goal.

Very often we underestimate our own abilities. As a result, we set goals that are too modest. Goals should have a lot of flexibility to be adjusted upward and a lot less flexibility to be adjusted downward. The ability to adjust goals upward easily enables progress to occur as fast as possible. The ability to adjust goals downward uneasily reduces the tendency to want to backslide at the first sign of difficulty; but having the flexibility to adjust downward can also prevent complete abandonment of a goal.

If you have first discovered your inspiration, your motivation, and your mission before you start setting goals, then you should not have any goals that conflict with your personal values. Such goals are unlikely to be achieved. Even if they were, it would be a hollow victory.

In addition to not conflicting with personal values, goals should not conflict with each other. One way of avoiding conflicting goals is to have a clear priority of goals. A first priority might be to reduce spending and increase savings. There might also be a goal of exercising more and losing weight. Both of those goals can be worked on simultaneously. However, joining a health club to promote more exercise may increase spending and reduce saving, which is in clear conflict with your first priority goal.

BECOMING WHEALTHY

Psychologists Robert Emmons and Laura King have demonstrated in a series of studies that conflicting goals create three main problems:
- **Worry** - The effort to reconcile competing or conflicting demands creates stress.
- **Lower productivity** - Conflict leads to confusion, which leads to paralysis, or at least inefficiency.
- **Physical and mental health problems** - Greater anxiety and depression are most common emotional problems, which lead to poorer health overall.

When we have an uncompleted task or an unreached goal, it's like the seven-note musical riff commonly known as "shave-and-a-haircut…two-bits." (You might recognize it as the banjo riff from *The Beverly Hillbillies,* right before a commercial break.)

When we have an unfinished task or unaccomplished goal, we can alleviate the distraction of it by making a written plan to complete the task or accomplish the goal. Once a plan is in place, our unconscious mind stops nagging our conscious mind and reverts to simple reminders to accomplish what has been promised.

Whenever we can take action that will help us achieve multiple goals simultaneously, it makes sense to do so. The essence of becoming whealthy is to take advantage of anything that can simultaneously improve your health and wealth. If dining out less often and eating at home will increase your savings and reduce your waistline at the same time, that's a double incentive to whip up something in the kitchen instead of making reservations. Viewed from another perspective, frequent dining out can reduce your wallet while it increases the butt that sits upon it.

Finally, every accomplished goal deserves a reward for reaching it. The reward should be commensurate with the difficulty of reaching that particular goal. Losing five pounds does not merit a new car, nor does losing one hundred pounds merit a mere bouquet of flowers.

If a goal is worthwhile, the change resulting from its accomplishment will be rewarding. The act of accomplishment will also be rewarding. The additional reward is the motivation to keep going during the task of reaching the goal. During that time, when the hard work is being done but the rewards are not yet forthcoming, we need all the help we can get to keep us moving forward.

BECOMING WHEALTHY

Becoming EFFICIENT

WHO AM I? by Unknown Author

I am your constant companion.
I am your greatest helper or your heaviest burden.
I will push you onward or drag you down to failure.
I am completely at your command.
Half the things you do, you might just as well turn over to me
and I will be able to do them quickly and correctly.
I am easily managed; you must merely be firm with me.
Show me exactly how you want something done,
and after a few lessons I will do it automatically.
I am the servant of all great men, and alas, of all failures as well.
Those who are great, I have made them great.
Those who are failures, I have made failures.
I am not a machine, though I work with the precision of
a machine, plus the intelligence of man.
You may run me for profit, or run me for ruin;
It makes no difference to me.
Take me, train me, be firm with me,
and I will put the world at your feet.
Be easy with me and I will destroy you.
Who am I? I am Habit!

BECOMING WHEALTHY

Every day around the world there are over 100 million women who, either intentionally or unknowingly, do additional physical work in order to avoid doing more mental work. There is a valid reason why these women trade one kind of work for another. Almost all of them would not change their current habit even if given another option.

These 100 million women are on "the pill," or more precisely, the combined oral contraceptive pill. The birth control pill has been available since 1960. It is the most successful contraceptive in history. The prescription calls for the woman to take a combination of estrogen and progestin in pill form daily for 21 days, then to abstain from the dosage for 7 days. Almost all prescriptions are packaged with 28 pills - 21 active pills and 7 placebos. The placebos are clearly identified in the packaging with a different color.

Women can choose not to take the placebos, though most do. The reason they choose to take a pill they don't need is habit. The physical work involved in taking a pill a day for a week is minimal; for most women it is simply part of a daily routine. What is actually harder is to remember to start taking the active pills after a week off. Most women (and men, too) would calculate that the mental effort to remember, combined with the ramifications of forgetting, make taking the placebo the smart choice. There is virtually no effort required to take a pill every day because it has been made into a habit.

Humans think in two different ways - one that is intuitive and automatic, the other that is rational and reflective. Psychologists refer to these methods of thinking as System 1 and System 2, respectively.

The automatic system is just that - it relies on instinct, rather than thought. When we react to a clap of thunder or a baby's laugh, we are using our automatic system. The reflective system is thoughtful and deliberate. You're using your reflective system while reading this book. Your native tongue is your automatic system regarding language. It takes years of training to take a second language from your reflective system to your automatic system. The goal of almost any learned skill is to raise that skill to the level where the exercise of that skill goes from being reflective to automatic.

We like to use our automatic system because it's a lot less work than using our reflective system. We also like to give ourselves credit for using our reflective systems when we are actually using our automatic systems.

When we watch TV news or read journals that agree with our point of view, we like to think we are being reflective, even though we are actually defaulting to our automatic systems. Reflective thinking involves *reflecting* on what the other side is saying, and that reflection requires some serious effort.

While humans aren't lazy, we are constantly seeking ways to perform a task with less effort. Most of man's inventions with moving parts are the result of this quest to do more work with less human effort. As part of this never-ending quest, any time we can move a task from our reflective to our automatic system, we are likely to do so.

Our habits are controlled by our automatic system. Our automatic system looks to make the everyday tasks of living as effortless as possible. The main reason we develop habits is so we don't have to think about what we're doing. Almost by definition, if you have to think about doing something, it isn't a habit. All those tasks you do in the course of a day - those that, once you've done them, you can't remember any of the specifics -

those are habits, and they are being handled by your automatic system.

Humans have an inherent mind-body conflict. Our bodies are built for performance, but our brains are always looking for ways to minimize energy consumption. Both body and brain have evolved this way over hundreds of thousands of years; we are not likely to change any time soon. As a species, humans are noteworthy for our physical endurance, but endurance depends on conserving energy, which is the brain's responsibility.

This mind-body conflict is apparent when we think about exercising. If you exercise regularly, it didn't come about naturally; you had to make a habit of it. Making a habit of regular exercise may not have reduced the physical energy required to exercise, but creating the habit of exercise practically eliminates the mental energy required to get started. When exercising isn't a habit, the hardest part of it is just getting started.

The brain can learn new things faster than it can unlearn old ones. For almost all of human history, taking it easy wasn't an option. Only in the last century or so have we created the technology that enables us to support ourselves while expending little energy.

Nothing has shaped you into the individual you are today more than your habits. More than forty percent of the actions a person takes in a typical day are habits. Yet nothing ever begins as a habit. At some point, you made conscious decisions about everything you do that would now be considered a habit. Once you stopped thinking about it, once you decided that choosing required too much effort, the behavior became automatic and a habit was born. If you are not as whealthy as you could be or would like to be, it is likely that some of your habits are at the root of the problem. Before we can change habits, though, we need to understand how they work.

The process of converting a sequence of actions into an automatic routine is known as *chunking*. Much of our day relies on our use of behavioral chunks. By the time you get to work in the morning, you have relied on dozens of behavioral chunks, from making coffee to brushing your teeth to driving out of your neighborhood.

Behavioral scientists believe our brain creates chunks because the brain is always looking for ways to reduce effort. The brain isn't lazy; it's just trying to be as efficient as possible. Our brain soaks up twenty percent of our total body energy, even when it isn't actively engaged in creating or problem-solving. Turning routines into habits is just the brain's way of conserving energy. An efficient brain also allows for a smaller brain, which any woman who has ever gone through childbirth can appreciate. A brain that doesn't have to think about how to walk can spend its energy on more lofty pursuits.

Our brains look for cues to tell it when to go into habit mode. Your brain's first cue in the morning is probably your alarm clock going off. Almost everything you do between the time you get up and the time you arrive at work is probably based on habits. Most days, nothing unusual happens, so your brain reinforces the habit. Occasionally, something unusual happens, and you are jolted out of the routine. One of the reasons we don't like to have our routines interrupted is that those interruptions require us to engage in unplanned thought.

Studies of the brain have revealed an important fact - our habits develop automatically, without conscious thought on our part. Anything that enables the body to work less will automatically be endorsed by the body. You don't have to give your stamp of approval for a habit to form. The habit will form of its own accord, as long as there is a routine that can be followed, there is something to cue that routine, and at the end of the routine there is positive reinforcement, or at least the absence of negative reinforcement.

Your body doesn't distinguish between good and bad habits. The problem is bad habits usually have better rewards than good habits. Spending is more rewarding than saving. Watching a ball game, while sitting on the sofa drinking beer and eating chips, definitely feels better at that moment than going jogging. The cues are also biased in favor of bad habits. Supermarkets put candy bars at the checkout counter and vegetables way in the back. Your TV remote is sitting right in front of you while your running shoes are hiding in the closet.

The good news is that good habits can become just as rewarding as bad ones. Our habits become familiar to us, and familiarity brings comfort. Good habits have just as much ability to become familiar and comforting as bad habits, and they can do so without any of the nasty side effects of bad habits.

Habits don't need our permission to form. If they did, most of us would have far fewer bad habits. Habits can seep into our consciousness, as well as being the product of a conscious choice. Once a behavior pattern becomes a habit, the brain wants to cling to it, even if it clashes with common sense. Samuel Johnson, the eighteenth century English writer said, "The chains of habit are too weak to be felt until they are too strong to be broken." Let's amend that to say the chains of habit can be broken, but it takes an effort to do so.

A habit begins with a cue, a triggering event. It ends with some positive reinforcement, a reward. In between is the routine itself. There are all kinds of cues coming at us constantly. All advertising is a cue. If the reward meets expectations, a habit is in the making. If you see the golden arches on the way home from work, that's a cue. When you enjoy a Big Mac and fries and don't have to cook that night, that's your reward. Since you pass those golden arches almost every day, it isn't hard to develop a fast food habit.

Advertising is more about psychology than marketing. For nearly a century, people who have succeeded in advertising have understood two basic rules to get people to buy something. There has to be a simple and obvious cue, and there have to be clearly defined rewards. An extension of that second rule is, don't sell features; sell benefits.

Habits are powerful, in large part, because they create neurological cravings in our brain. As habits become stronger and we come to expect a reward by engaging in a certain habit, our brain responds to the reward before it is even received. The expectation of something pleasurable gets dopamine flowing in our brain, sometimes triggered by the routine, but with strong habits it is triggered by the cue itself. We aren't much different from Pavlov's dogs in the sense that we can be programmed to expect a reward and react to it before it even arrives.

Habits are formed when a cue, a routine, and a reward are mated with a craving that powers the loop. Most cravings involve the release of dopamine in our brain. Dopamine is the chemical that is released whenever we experience something pleasurable. We love dopamine, so we tend to do over and over anything that causes the brain to release dopamine. Everyone is different, so people vary in what stimuli release dopamine. For some, it's gambling; for some, it's exercise; for some, it's shopping; for some, it's building wealth.

It's one thing to start an exercise program; it's quite another to turn it into a habit. Most people who maintain a regular exercise program do so because there is a reward they begin to crave. A good workout will produce endorphins, a group of chemicals released by the brain. Endorphins are most frequently produced as response to pain or stress, like the physical stress and pain from a good workout.

In addition to decreased feelings of pain, secretion of endorphins leads to feelings of euphoria, modulation of appetite, release of sex hormones, and enhancement of the immune response. With high endorphin levels, we feel less pain and fewer negative effects of stress. If you thought people who exercise a lot were just crazy, now you know they get high on a non-addictive chemical with only positive side effects.

Anticipating the reward is what creates cravings, and cravings are what create habits. This pattern is the same for good habits and bad habits. For those who exercise regularly, the reward of an endorphin rush might be sufficient. They might also enjoy the reward of how they look in the mirror or the number that shows up on the scale.

The creation of a new habit begins with the creation of a craving. Most of us know that the best way to avoid developing a craving for something that's bad for us is to never try it in the first place. That method may work for "acquired" habits like gambling or heroin addiction. However, it's hard to avoid cravings for which we are biologically hot-wired, like eating, drinking, and sex. Some temptations can be avoided; others must simply be overcome.

Bad habits can never truly be extinguished, but there are ways to change them. The most effective way to change a habit is to keep the cue, to keep the reward, but change to the routine in the middle.

Alcoholism is more than a habit; it's a medically recognized addiction. Over the years, the most successful method of treating alcoholism has been Alcoholics Anonymous (AA).

AA focuses on the habits surrounding alcohol use. AA helps alcoholics identify cues that trigger the craving for a drink and the rewards they feel they receive from drinking. The cues and rewards don't change, but the routine in the middle does. The routine used to be to drink. For most in AA, that routine is replaced by either seeking support or lending it through meetings.

Once you become aware of how your habits develop and are reinforced, you are well on your way to changing those habits. Simply knowing that you don't have to give up the reward can be a great motivator to change the routine, which is the key to changing the habit. What is required is the desire and will to change the routine.

An individual's personal desire and will to change can be enough on most days, when everything is going on as routine. It is when we get thrown out of our routine, especially by something stressful, that we revert back to our old habits.

Because the people with whom we associate can have a huge influence on our behavior, it's important to look at how they might be influencing the habits we develop. If our associates have bad habits, there's a good chance we will develop some of those same habits. In general, if you hang around with people who behave better than you do, you will begin to behave better. The opposite, of course, is also true.

BECOMING WHEALTHY

Some habits matter more than others. Such habits are ones that, when they change, other habits change as well. These are known as *keystone habits*, and changing one of these for the better can have ripple effects in many other areas.

Exercise is considered a keystone habit. Once people begin an exercise habit, they reconsider other habits that are likely to undo the progress made by exercise. They begin to eat better, get more sleep, and reduce or eliminate drugs and alcohol. Because they feel better physically, they become more productive at work, they feel less stressed, and they become better company with friends and family. A positive change in a keystone habit pays unforeseen benefits in areas that might seem to be unrelated.

Habits begin with a choice, and America has more choices for just about everything than any other place on earth. In collectivist societies, like Japan, people think in terms of "we" first and "I" second. In the U.S., we put liberty and individualism on such a high pedestal, we think in terms of "I" first and "we" second.

With an individualist mentality, you are less likely to consider the adverse effect your habit might have on others. With a collectivist mentality, your first thoughts are how a habit might affect others. If the effect on others is negative, you are less likely to let a bad habit develop.

The collectivist mentality might be thought of as peer pressure. West Point Cadets are required to adhere to the Cadet Honor Code, which states: "A cadet will not lie, cheat, steal, or tolerate those who do." That level of peer pressure means that very few cadets ever develop such bad habits. It isn't the external pressure alone that keeps people in such situations on the straight and narrow. The desire to be accepted and respected in a group is a powerful incentive to keep one's bad habits to a minimum.

People who feel a sense of duty to others, or even to themselves, are less likely to develop bad habits and are more likely to develop good ones. This sense of duty acts as a governor on our natural desire to seek immediate gratification without concern for longer-term consequences. Studies in several countries have shown that as this sense of duty in a society declines, the bad habits and other harmful activities of individuals increase.

In his 1941 book *Escape from Freedom*, social theorist Erich Fromm argues that freedom is composed of two complementary parts - freedom *from* and freedom *to*. True freedom requires both, though each individual and culture may put greater emphasis on one over the other. In the context of habits, we want to believe we have the freedom to choose our own habits, even if they are bad ones. We also want the freedom from the consequences of the bad habits of others. This tension is constant in any free society.

While habits provide consistency, they are the enemy of flexibility. If habits were flexible, people would be ditching bad habits as soon as they recognized them as such. When the human brain decides to create a habit, it does not distinguish between a good one and a bad one. Since bad habits tend to have an advantage, they are easier to make and are harder to break than good ones.

When you think of your bad habits, they may give you pleasure, but they don't make you happy. Happiness involves a holistic experience, which means happiness depends on the total effect of an activity. A bad habit, like smoking or overeating, may bring pleasure at the moment of consumption, but the overall effect is to make the user unhappy, because the overall effect is negative. Happiness is not generated from a negative.

It's unlikely you've ever heard of Vilfredo Pareto (1848-1923). He was an Italian engineer, sociologist, economist, political scientist, and philosopher. His greatest contribution is probably the theory that bears his name, the Pareto Principle. The reason you probably don't know of Pareto or his principle is because the more common name for the Pareto Principle is the 80/20 Rule. Across the spectrum of human endeavors, there is a consistent pattern that 20% of the input is responsible for 80% of the output.

The 80/20 Rule is so important because, like many of the keys to success, it is counter-intuitive. We tend to think that equal inputs should have equal outputs and that when identical efforts do not yield identical results, there is an unfairness to the system that must be rectified. Instead of focusing our efforts on the productive 20%, we spend too much time and effort in an almost always futile effort to lift the bottom 80% to the level of the top 20%.

Expanding upon Pareto's principle in the 1940s, Joseph Juran developed a method of quality management that centered on the theory that 80% of quality problems are caused by 20% of the causes. Juran also argued that human problems - mainly a resistance to change - were at the core of most quality problems.

If we know from Pareto that 20% of inputs create 80% of outputs, and if we know from Juran that 80% of problems are caused by 20% of causes, we also know that we can greatly improve who we are by focusing on these two areas.

BECOMING WHEALTHY

We all have certain strengths that have served us well throughout our lives. These strengths probably came naturally to us, so we tend to take them for granted, which is another way of saying we undervalue them. Also, if we will admit it, we all have some glaring weaknesses that tend to erase much of the progress that our strengths could be providing to us.

To become as efficient as you can become, your efforts should be focused as follows:

1. Recognize, develop, and utilize your strengths to their fullest advantage. "Lead with your strength" is not just some slogan; it is a cornerstone to becoming whealthy.
2. Recognize your most glaring weaknesses and then work to minimize the damage they do to you. You are unlikely to turn a glaring weakness into a strength, nor is it a good use of your limited time, energy, and willpower to try. You can, however, reduce such a liability substantially.
3. Recognize your remaining mild strengths and weaknesses for what they are and ignore them. The return on investment from trying to improve in these areas is almost non-existent. Your time is much better spent on steps 1 and 2.

According to Richard Koch, author of *The 80/20 Principle*, we should do the following to make the most of the 80/20 rule:

- focus on exceptional productivity; ignore average efforts
- look for short cuts
- maximize control over our lives with minimum effort
- be selective, not exhaustive

- become excellent in a few things, not merely good in many
- delegate and outsource as much as possible
- choose careers with extraordinary care
- become self-employed if possible
- only do what you do best and enjoy most
- look for ironies, oddities, and abnormalities to exploit
- look at everything through the 80/20 lens

Focusing your efforts where desired change is most likely to occur will greatly simplify your life. You will spend far less time on your efforts, and the results will exceed whatever you are currently doing. Because time is the one resource we all get an equal share of every day, the differences between us begin with how we use that time.

You can begin by reducing or eliminating some of the low-value uses of your time. These time wasters include: what others tell you to do, what you don't do well, what has always been done that way, and what you don't enjoy doing.

With the time you save from eliminating low-value uses, you can reallocate to high value uses, which include: what you've always wanted to do, what advances your overall purpose in life, and what falls under the category of now or never.

The overall theme of the 80/20 principle as it applies to your time is you want to identify the times when you are happiest and increase them as much as possible. At the same time, you want to identify the times when you are the unhappiest and reduce them as much as possible.

Kaizen was created in Japan following World War II. The word Kaizen roughly translates to "continuous improvement." It comes from the Japanese words "kai", which means change or to correct, and "zen", which means good. Kaizen is a useful approach to improve one's personal circumstances. Take the spirit of Kaizen and apply it to your own personal approach to improve - step by step, little by little.

There is an old saying - "Once you think you have arrived, you have already started your descent." There is another old saying - "If it ain't broke, don't fix it." The spirit of Kaizen suggests that there is *always* something to learn and that there are always ways to improve. It is better to prevent problems than to have to fix them later. No matter how good things may seem now, there is always room for improvement.

Studies done of runners in the annual New York Marathon have uncovered some fascinating data on our endurance, not over distance, but over years. The studies have shown that, starting at age 19, runners get faster every year until they reach their peak around age 27. While those ages are not surprising, this fact is. Runners who peak at the typical age of 27 do not fall back to their age 19 pace until they are in their early 60's! The amazing finding is that, not only are we capable of running longer distances than almost any other animal, we have the ability to do it well for decades.

Jack Kirk, a legendary runner who lived to be 100 and ran arduous races until the age of 96, said "You don't stop running because you get old. You get old because you stop running."

We have an inherent conflict between our minds and our bodies. Our bodies are built for performance, as evidenced by the variety of amazing feats performed at every Olympiad. Our brains, on the other hand, are always looking for ways to do things more efficiently. Our problem today is we have to actually fight the natural instinct to conserve energy because the sedentary lifestyle it has created is now the biggest threat to our individual survival.

Nearly all of the biggest killers in the Western world - heart disease, stroke, diabetes, hypertension, depression, as well as many forms of cancer - were virtually unknown to our ancestors. They didn't have cures for these diseases; they had a preventative. It was regular, vigorous exercise.

In the 21st century, we need a new, rapid evolution in our brain's way of thinking. Our bodies are as good or better than they've ever been, if we take care of them. The new efficiency is not in conserving energy, but in consuming it. When we consume energy through physical activity, we create more of it.

I invest 6 hours a week to exercise. The average person has a resting pulse rate of 72 bpm (beats per minute). Mine is about 60 bpm. At 72 bpm, a person's heart beats 725,760 times in a week. At 60 bpm, a person's heart beats 604,800 times in a week.

If I exercise 6 hours per week, my heart will beat an extra 32,400 times due to the exercise. I invest 32,400 beats to save 120,960 beats (725,760 - 604,800). My heart beats 88,560 fewer times in a week than it would if I didn't exercise and had a normal rate of 72 bpm. If we each have a predetermined number of heartbeats, the 88,560 heartbeats I save every week adds 24.6 hours to my life - every single week.

I make a weekly investment in the habit of exercise with 6 hours and 32,400 heartbeats. My weekly return is 24.6 hours and 88,560 heartbeats. Exercise for me is more than good habit; it's an investment with a spectacular return.

Becoming SMARTER & WISER

THOUGHT by Berton Braley

*You say "I think" ten times a day
Or fifteen times, or twenty
And even more. Well, anyway
You sure repeat it plenty.
But pause and ponder half a wink
And start your brain-cells clinking;
"I Think" you say, but do you Think
Or only Think you're thinking?*

*How often is the thing you've thought
Out of yourself created
And not a dictum you've been taught
And simply imitated?
Into a reverie you sink
And like an owl you're blinking,
But do you actually Think,
Or only Think you're thinking?*

*"I Think" you say - and ladle out
Some fusty old opinion
That probably was known about
In old King Tut's dominion.
Do new ideas ever slink
Into your cranium's chinking?
I wonder - do you really think
Or only Think you're thinking?*

*Traditions, customs, fill your head
And some of them have virtue,*

BECOMING WHEALTHY

But most of them have long been dead;
They fester there and hurt you.
Son, chuck that clutter in the drink,
Wake up - don't sit there blinking!
Wake up! And then perhaps you'll Think
And not just think you're thinking!

How many choices did you make today? It's not a question you likely think about much, so take a minute to think about it now. What time did you choose to get up? When the alarm went off, did you choose to get up right away, or did you choose instead to hit the snooze button? What did you choose to eat for breakfast, or did you choose to skip breakfast because you hit the snooze once too often? What did you choose to wear to work? What brand of toothpaste, deodorant, soap, and cologne did you choose?

You make a dozen or more choices before you ever leave the house to go to work. You also make several choices on the way to work. What route will you take? What will you listen to on the commute? Should you return the rude gesture that guy just flashed you? We could spend several pages reviewing your choices in a typical day. You can see from this brief illustration that it's easy to get worn out from choosing and deciding before you ever even get to the office. We surrender many daily choices to habit precisely to avoid getting worn out by 9am.

We consider freedom of choice to be the cornerstone of all human rights. Consider what we consider to be the most egregious violations of human rights. People living under dictatorships are denied the right to choose their leaders. Whenever we feel outrage over some violation of human rights, a violation of the right to choose is almost always at the heart of it.

When someone is sent to prison, perhaps the most difficult part of the transition to prison life is adjusting to virtually no freedom of choice. Inmates in most prisons do not get to choose what they wear, what they eat, with whom they associate, or what they do each hour of the day. The differences between lower and higher security prisons are less about physical confinement and more about reducing freedom of choice. Freedom of choice is the most valued freedom, so it is naturally the one that is taken away first when someone violates the laws of society.

We want the freedom to choose, but we don't want the act of choosing to become overwhelming. Everyone has an instinct for his/her own sweet spot when it comes to choosing. When you have too little freedom of choice, you feel trapped or degraded as a person. When you have too many choices, the benefits of having many options are overwhelmed by the task of having to come up with what you hope will be the best choice.

A study on retirement plan offerings revealed how more choices can vex consumers. The study looked at 647 retirement plans offered by a variety of employers, which encompassed 793,749 employees. The plans offered from 2 to 59 different mutual fund choices within the plan. Each employee was responsible for choosing the funds to invest in for his/her account. The rates of participation for the plans broke down as follows:

Funds Offered	Employee Participation Rate
1-5	73%
6-30	71%
31-35	69%
36-40	66%
41-59	63%

As the number of choices increased, participation decreased!

Few employers today offer guidance to employees on how to invest for retirement. There are two main reasons for this lack of guidance. Employers are rarely qualified to offer such advice. More important, employers are afraid of assuming liability for the poor performance of any recommendations. Employees are left to figure out for themselves how to allocate their contributions to their retirement plans.

With more and more funds to choose from, the task of choosing the right ones becomes harder. This study showed three negative effects of increasing options. First, the participation rate went down. Roughly 10% of employees decided it was too much trouble to participate at all when the choices increased dramatically. Second, the average amount contributed to the plans declined significantly. Employees were less willing to risk their money on a choice that might be wrong. Third, as fund choices (especially equity funds) increased, the percentage of money allocated to equity funds decreased.

For long-term investing, equity funds are necessary to provide growth that will outpace inflation. The well-intentioned idea of offering more choice to employees to help them accumulate more for retirement had the opposite effect. One in ten dropped out because of the increasing choice, and the rest invested less and invested more conservatively than their situations warranted.

We've already discussed the importance of setting goals as a prerequisite to becoming whealthy. Goals are also necessary if you are to make good choices.

Good decisions require you to first figure out your goals and then to prioritize them. The next step is to array your options and evaluate how each option is likely to help you achieve your most important goals. Once you make your choice, you then follow up to see how your choice is performing toward reaching your goals. If the choice isn't working out, either another choice needs to be made, or if no choice exists to help you reach your goals, a re-evaluation of the goals themselves becomes necessary.

Choosing begins with a question - two questions, actually - "What do I need?" and "What do I want?" Our ability to choose wisely hinges on our ability to:
a) understand what we need,
b) understand the difference between true needs and mere desires,
c) understand what we want and why we want it.

Columnist George Will has said that Americans define a need as a 48-hour old want; there is a lot of truth there. Delayed gratification is not our strong suit. By elevating a want to a need we relieve ourselves of the stigma of having no willpower. Tending to needs is never considered selfish. Indulging in wants, especially when needs are going unmet or when one lacks the resources, leads to self-loathing and outside disapproval.

The technical term for measurement of meeting wants and/or needs is *utility*. There are three types of utility involved when we evaluate how satisfied we are with our choices:

- **Expected Utility**. Our choices begin here. Expected utility can be hard to gauge if we have had no prior experience in that area. There is a saying that the two happiest days in a boat owner's life are the day he buys it and the day he sells it. The truth of that statement is a strong indicator that the expected utility from owning a boat is greater than the next listed utility.
- **Experienced Utility**. This utility is what you actually feel when you are in the middle of the experience. For the boat owner, the experienced utility when cruising on a lake on a beautiful day is very high. The experienced utility of owning a boat also includes the effort to get the boat to and from the lake, the cost to transport the boat, and the maintenance and storage of the boat. For many, the experienced utility involves ten hours of work for one hour of pleasure, which varies greatly from the expected utility.
- **Remembered Utility**. Psychologist Daniel Kahneman has studied the field of utilities and has made some interesting findings. Among those findings is that what we remember about a past experience is determined by two things: how the experience felt when it was at its peak (best or worst) and how it felt when the experience ended. The boat owner who keeps his boat has likely had some really *memorable* days on the lake and is sad that the season is over. The boat owner who sells his boat has some really vivid memories of enormous expenses, no storage facilities, and a really hot day sitting on the interstate instead of the lake because the towing vehicle overheated.

BECOMING WHEALTHY

According to Kahneman, the experiencing self answers the question, "How does it feel now?" The remembering self answers the question, "How was it, on the whole?" The remembering self is sometimes wrong, but the remembering self is the scorekeeper and governs what we learn from living.

The remembering self is full of biases, too. When you make a choice, you don't want to be proven wrong in that choice. Even when your experienced utility does not meet the expected utility, your remembered utility may be upgraded in order to avoid the feeling that you screwed up.

Remembered utility is one reason why people remember the past more fondly than they felt about that period when they were actually experiencing it. Many people look back nostalgically at their high school days, forgetting the awkwardness, the peer pressure, and the insecurities, they endured at the time. The gauze of memory tends to filter out the impurities of the past, leaving us with pleasant, if inaccurate memories.

Such a filtering can be good if it brings comfort to an old person. The problem occurs when such distortions cause people to want to return to the "good old days," which were never as good as they remember them. As the French writer Madame d'Epinay put it, "One sees the past better than it was; one finds the present worse than it is; one hopes for a future happier than it will be."

In order to be able to say we know what we want, the expected utility, experienced utility, and remembered utility all need to meet expectations and be reasonably close together. Overestimating expected utility will lead to disappointment in experienced utility; underestimating it means you may not make that choice at all, bypassing an opportunity. If remembered utility is higher than experienced utility, you are likely to repeat a previous choice and be disappointed by the actual results. Such disappointment is a common result from attempting to relive the past.

As Dale Carnegie said, "Success is getting what you want and happiness is wanting what you get." Experiencing success *and* happiness, to get what you want *and* want what you get, is the ultimate reward when expected utility, experienced utility, and remembered utility are all in sync.

Since we are talking about utilities, there is another area where that word is used - the law of marginal utility. The law of marginal utility states: if you have a lot of something, one more unit of that thing doesn't have much of an impact.

For example, if you have ten million dollars, an additional ten dollars doesn't do much for you; the *utility* you get from the extra ten is *marginal*. On the other hand, if all you have is ten dollars, an extra ten dollars can make the difference whether or not you will eat today.

Economists like to think that people are rational robots and that the person with ten million dollars will place the same value on ten additional dollars as would a person with only ten total dollars. We know from our own personal experiences that we make different choices based on how much of something we have.

We have all been in a situation where we were worried about running out of gas. You may have been in an unfamiliar area that was sparsely populated, and you had no idea how far it was to the next gas station. To prevent running out of gas, you slowed down to 40 mph, turned off the A/C, and coasted whenever possible. Just when you thought you were about to run dry, an Exxon sign appeared over the horizon. Once your tank was full, you floored the gas pedal to make up for lost time. When you had little gas, every drop was precious, and you chose to be conservative. When you had plenty of gas, you no longer chose to be conservative. That's how the law of marginal utility works.

It may not surprise you that animals that view threats as more urgent than opportunities have a better chance to survive and reproduce. Put another way, while eating is important, the higher priority is not to be eaten.

Humans are animals, too. We have an instinct that tells us to fear loss more than to desire gain. Numerous studies have shown that people generally dislike a loss twice as much as they like a gain of comparable size. This loss aversion has been bred into us over millions of years. In modern times, it can prompt us to make some bad choices.

Most of the choices we make in life are mixed, in the sense that there is both a risk of loss and an opportunity for gain. This is certainly true in investing and could serve as the definition of investing itself. How we evaluate potential gains and losses determines what we do. Even when we accurately evaluate the potential gains and losses of a decision, how we feel toward those gains and losses will affect our decision.

Here is a simple test to measure your loss aversion. There is to be a coin toss. If the coin shows tails, you will lose $100. If the coin shows heads, you will gain $150. Will you accept the bet? What if the stakes were a $10 loss or a $15 gain. Would your decision change? What if the amounts were a $10,000 loss or a $15,000 gain?

If you are like most people, you would look at the fact that there is a 50-50 chance of heads or tails. You would then look at the amounts in question. You would likely accept the possibility of a $10 loss for an equal chance at a $15 gain. However, when it came to the bet where you could gain $15,000 or lose $10,000, you would almost certainly decline, even though the odds of winning are exactly the same in both bets.

In order to get you to gamble with the higher stakes, the stakes have to move more in your favor. For most people, when the prize for winning is at least twice as big as the penalty for losing, they will make the bet, assuming they can actually afford the loss. In this example, if you could afford to lose $10,000, the chance to win $20,000 is likely to motivate you to accept the bet.

When someone makes a bet like this one and loses, they can become very loss averse. People who invest in stocks that drop in value may become so loss averse that they stop investing at all in stocks, which can be detrimental to their chances of becoming whealthy. Conversely, when people make bets like this one and win, they may become overconfident, and their aversion to loss may become suppressed. They may take bigger and bigger risks until the odds finally catch up to them. Loss aversion is one of those innate characteristics that we need to control, but never totally suppress.

Whenever we contemplate a financial decision, we look for a reference point, an *anchor*. This anchor helps us determine whether or not we are getting a good deal. People buy items on sale because they use the non-sale price as an anchor. If a dress is normally $79 and if JC Penney puts it on sale for $49, people are likely to buy it. The anchor price of $79 makes them feel as if they're getting a good deal. If JC Penney set an everyday price of $45 for the same dress, they would sell fewer of them.

People would not have an anchor to determine if they were getting a good deal or not.

If you've ever gone into a nice restaurant and looked at the wine list, you have probably seen a bottle or two priced in the stratosphere. The restaurant would be happy to sell you their most expensive wine, but that's not why it's on the list. The purpose of those labels is to make the next tier of wines look like bargains in comparison. That second tier is both very profitable and high-volume, but it's the wines on the first tier serving as anchors that makes them so.

Your decision to buy or not buy something is often determined by how the offer is framed. *Framing* is a term used to describe the context in which a proposition is made.

If you've ever made a purchase where there were different prices for cash and credit, such as a gas station, you probably saw the price difference framed with a term like "discount for cash." What you almost certainly didn't see was a term like "surcharge for credit." The first framing seems to offer a reward for cash without a penalty for credit; the second seems to offer a penalty for credit without a reward for cash. With the first framing, cash purchases are encouraged without discouraging credit purchases. With the second framing, credit purchases are discouraged without encouraging cash purchases. Even if the prices are exactly the same in both circumstances, framing the difference as a discount, rather than a surcharge, will result in substantially higher sales in both categories.

If you've shopped for a new car in recent years, you may have been surprised when the salesperson encouraged you to take the car home with you, even though you had made it very clear you were not ready to strike a deal. The sales person was relying on the *endowment effect* to work its magic on you.

Once we take possession of something; physically, mentally, or even symbolically, it assumes greater value to us than it did before we took possession. When we take possession of the new car, even if it's "just overnight," the endowment effect kicks in for us. We are far more reluctant to turn the car back in than we were when we merely took it for a test drive at the dealership.

Anchoring and the endowment effect also work against us when we want to sell our own possessions. If you paid $250,000 for your house, that is your anchor. The thought of selling it for $200,000 is repugnant to you. Even if you paid $150,000 for your house, and the value at its peak was $250,000, the thought of selling it for $200,000 is still repugnant. For our own property, the anchor tends to become whatever its highest value was, regardless of when that occurred.

The other factor working against us when we sell our house is the endowment effect. Few possessions mean as much to us or express who we are as much as our homes. As a result, we value them far more than others do. Even if we get a good price, there is still a sense of loss. The buyer is merely buying *a house*; we are selling *our home*. One of the most important roles of a realtor is to help us get past our anchoring and endowment effects and to set a price that the market will respond to positively.

If contempt for politicians is so low, why do we re-elect 85% of them, on average? The answer most people will give is that, even though all politicians are crooked, *my* representative is not. We have a similar opinion about our education system. Most Americans feel that our education system, in general, is poor. Yet their opinion of *their* neighborhood school is overwhelmingly positive.

The feeling that our own representatives and our own schools are good while the others are not is an example of the endowment effect. The endowment effect can lead to another flaw in our decision-making process, *status quo bias*.

When we are faced with a multitude of choices, especially when the pros and cons of those choices are not crystal clear, we choose the default option, the status quo. Part of the reason for our preference for the status quo is the pain we know we will feel if we make a change and if it doesn't work. If we change our congressman and if the new one ends up indicted for something, we will feel worse than if we left the old congressman in office and he were indicted. We kick ourselves when we make a change and it doesn't work, even though we have no way of knowing if the status quo would have been any better.

We are all familiar with the old phrase, "in for a penny, in for a pound." The phrase was coined in England more than 300 years ago, and it basically means that if you're on the hook for a small amount, you might as well get on the hook for a big amount in the hopes of not suffering a loss. In remembering occasions when you heard that phrase uttered, you may also remember that the additional gambit rarely paid off.

Imagine that you are on a game show and that you have won $10,000. You are eligible for the next phase, in which you can receive an extra $5,000 automatically, or you can flip a coin to either receive $10,000 more or nothing more. Which option would you choose?

Imagine that you are on the same game show and that you have lost $10,000. (On this particular game show, when you lose, you actually have to pay them the loss out of your own pocket.) In the next phase of the game, you are given a choice - accept a reduction of your loss to $5,000 and quit, or flip a coin to either owe the original $10,000 or owe nothing at all. Which option would you choose?

If you are like the overwhelming majority of people, in the first scenario you take the guaranteed increase of $5,000 and quit. If you're like that same overwhelming majority, in the second scenario you flip the coin to try to dig yourself out of a hole.

Both scenarios are virtually the same. In both, the default option makes you $5,000 better off than you were. If you flip the coin and win, you are $10,000 better off; if you flip and lose, you are no better off. The only difference is in the starting point.

When we are ahead in the game, we become cautious and want to consolidate our winnings. When we are behind in the game, we will take on a lot of additional risk in the hopes of getting back to even. The in-for-a-penny, in-for-a-pound mindset is known as the *sunk-cost fallacy*. It asserts that when our money is already sunk into something - whether it's a gamble, an investment, or a disappointing relative - we are inclined to keep throwing good money after bad in the hope of salvaging our sunk costs.

Another aspect of sunk-cost fallacy asserts that, once we have sunk money into a particular investment, we are reluctant to sink money into anything that might make that original investment irrelevant. Many companies are slow to upgrade equipment, such as computers, when they've recently invested money in that current equipment. To upgrade the equipment now would make them feel like the previous investment was a waste of money. The only factor that should be considered in such cases is whether the *new* investment will generate a rate of return that justifies that investment.

There will be times when we don't get to make the choice we want, or the choice we make turns out to be a disappointment. The unpleasant experience of being caught between conflicting forces or feelings is known as *cognitive dissonance*, a classic example of which is Aesop's fable of the fox and the grapes. The fox desires some grapes, but finds he is unable to reach them. To ease his frustration, the fox convinces himself that the grapes were probably sour and that he wouldn't have enjoyed them anyway.

Because of the abundance of choices we have available, we reject far more than we accept. In order to keep our cumulative rejections from driving us crazy, once we take ownership of our choice, we automatically increase our rating of it (the endowment effect) while downgrading our ratings of our rejected options. Whenever a decision is unencumbered, important, and irreversible, the potential for cognitive dissonance exists.

Anchors, framing, endowment effects, status quo bias, sunk cost fallacy, and cognitive dissonance are examples of how we can be manipulated into certain choices without even being aware of it. Psychologically, there are all kinds of ways we impede our chances of becoming whealthy, and, most of the time, we are totally oblivious to them. Becoming aware is a necessary prerequisite to becoming whealthy.

People whose goal is perfection in every decision are known as *maximizers*. Maximizers tend to be frustrated and unhappy because reality almost never meets their goals and expectations. They will spend a great deal of time on the decision-making process, and they will make some excellent decisions as a result. Unfortunately, they will never fully enjoy the fruits of their labors because their assessment is based on relative standards, not absolute one. Their assessment is based relative to perfection, which is impossible to achieve.

Satisficers are the opposite of maximizers. They do not expect perfection from themselves, and they don't expect their decisions to be perfect. Satisficers set absolute standards, and when those standards have been met, they won't spend additional resources for incremental improvements. Satisficers are well aware of the point of diminishing returns; whereas, maximizers blow way past that point because they are obsessed with perfection.

Maximizers may make some better individual decisions than satisficers, but they also don't make some decisions that need to be made. They are preoccupied with making the best decision every time. Satisficers may give up a little on the quality of their decisions, but they more than make up for it in quantity. Satisficers will take care of all the business that needs to be taken care of and will still have a life.

Maximizers also suffer from an affliction that satisficers do not – buyer's remorse. Maximizers pay a price in mental anguish that satisficers rarely do. They also usually end up worse off financially than satisficers. Satisficers see the big picture and know when it's time to allocate resources to more productive endeavors.

Maximizers are micro, not macro, and so they lose out on many opportunities because they can't see past their current obsession. Going back to the 80/20 rule, satisficers are for more likely than maximizers to focus on the 20% of inputs that generates 80% of outcomes and ignore the rest.

When confronted with a dizzying array of choices, we are far better off setting reasonable expectations of ourselves and our ultimate selection and then moving on after our decision has been made. We may make mistakes, perhaps even more than the maximizers, but we shouldn't allow them to bother us or diminish our enjoyment of our ultimate selection.

Since every choice involves acceptance *and* rejection, every choice has trade-offs, or what economists call *opportunity costs*. When you decide to get the house painted, the money spent on that project means you don't have the opportunity to take a vacation or buy a home entertainment system.

The more choices we have, the higher the opportunity costs, since there are more opportunities that must be foregone. As opportunity costs increase, so do the chances that we will regret the decision we've made. When you have to choose between only two items, you can feel pretty confident you've made the right decision - at least a 50% chance, statistically speaking. When you have to choose between ten items, there is one chance to be right and nine chances to be wrong - a 10% chance you won't regret your choice.

The freedom to choose is one of our most cherished freedoms. But freedom of choice, like all freedoms, isn't free. There are psychological factors that most people are unaware of that impede their ability to make good decisions and to be comfortable with their choices. Even when you understand the mechanics and the pitfalls of the decision-making process, the tendency to obsess about what was on the path not taken can devalue even the best of choices.

There at least 300 acknowledged human emotions. Emotions come from the right brain, which is also where our creative thinking takes place. Emotions, along with creative thinking, are what make humans different from animals.

Emotions are triggered by a variety of stimuli, such as your mood, personality, or disposition, and by hormones such as dopamine, adrenaline, and serotonin. Instinctual emotions, such as fright from a sudden lightning strike nearby, originate in the amygdala, a primitive part of the brain obsessed with survival. Cognitive emotions, like pride or love, originate in the pre-frontal cortex, an advanced part of our brain that exists in only a handful of other animals, like dolphins and chimps.

Instinctual emotions are necessary for survival, and it would be dangerous to try to circumvent them, even if we could. We will limit our discussion to cognitive emotions, the ones that we create in our minds. They are the emotions that, more than anything else, can keep us from becoming whealthy.

Any positive or negative emotion can be used as an excuse to spend money, get drunk, or eat an entire cheesecake. We will focus in this chapter on those emotions that are likely to cause you the most trouble in your quest to become whealthy.

In the 1970's, social scientists subscribed to two ideas about human nature. First, people are rational by default, and their thinking is normally sound. Second, emotions like fear, hatred, greed, and love explain those occasions when people do not behave rationally. Daniel Kahneman, a psychologist who won the Nobel Prize in economics for his pioneering work in how people behave with money, was one of the first to challenge the generally accepted notion of humans as rational beings. In a career of more than four decades, Kahneman, along with his partner, Amos Tversky, proved that people are not inherently rational and that emotions are a big reason why they aren't.

When we think of ways in which emotions affect our health and wealth, we often think in terms of actions we took based on emotions that came back to hurt us. While we all have a long list of such events in our lives, emotions can affect us even when we don't act on them.

Your body responds to the way you think and feel, which is often referred to as the *mind-body connection*. When you are stressed, anxious, or upset, your body tries to tell you that something isn't right. You may develop headaches, muscle aches, high blood pressure, nausea, or any number of symptoms that can be traced back to your emotional state.

Poor emotional health weakens your immune system. You may also act in ways detrimental to your health, such as drinking too much or failing to get exercise because it's too hard at that moment.

Positive emotions can have the opposite effect. Gratitude, charity, and humor are examples of emotions that make us feel good and release endorphins, the same chemical mixture that the brain releases during orgasm. The old saying that laughter is the best medicine has been proven to be medically valid. Positive emotions can offset much of the damage caused by negative emotions, provided the negative emotions haven't festered long enough to cause major health problems.

Changes, whether good or bad, can be stressful and can be a trigger for a plethora of emotions. Most of the greatest stressors in our lives involve major changes - loss of a spouse, job change, birth of a child, marriage, divorce, sudden financial gain or loss, serious injury or disease, and many others.

Major changes force us to change certain habits, and the resulting stress can release a torrent of emotions. The emotions released may also conflict with each other, further increasing the stress. Many of us who have lost a loved one after a long illness have felt the conflicting emotions of sadness over death, while at the same time feeling relief that both the person's suffering and our burden of care have been lifted.

Martin Seligman, Ph.D., one of the preeminent experts in the field of positive psychology, offers this appraisal on the value of a positive attitude: "When it comes to our health, there are essentially four things under our control: the decision not to smoke, a commitment to exercise, the quality of our diet, and our level of optimism. And optimism is at least as beneficial as the others." Scientific studies have confirmed that positive emotions have a positive effect, not only on a person's immune system, but also on the ability to recover from setbacks in health.

A study conducted jointly by the University of Kansas and Gallup looked at data from 150,000 adults from 140 countries providing a representative sampling of 95 percent of the world's population. Participants reported emotions such as happiness, enjoyment, worry, and sadness. They answered questions about physical health and whether basic needs like food, water, clothing, shelter, and physical safety were adequately met.

According to the findings of this study, positive emotions are unmistakably linked to better health, even when a lack of basic needs is taken into account. Most strikingly, the association between emotions and physical health was more powerful than the connection between health and basic human physical requirements, like adequate nourishment. Even without food or shelter, positive emotions were shown to boost health. In fact, this association was strongest in the poorest countries.

Albert Schweitzer, philosopher, physician, missionary, and recipient of the Nobel Peace Prize, said, "Success is not the key to happiness; happiness is the key to success." Dale Carnegie, author of one of the best-selling books of all time, *How to Win Friends and Influence People*, said, "Success is getting what you want; happiness is wanting what you get." These two quotations point out two important points about what is probably the most sought-after emotion. First, happiness is both a starting point *and* a destination. Second, happiness is not something we find; it's something we create.

There is hardly a soul alive who has not said, at some point, words to the effect: "If I only had/made (fill-in-the-blank), I'd be happy." We begin this habit in childhood. We all just knew that if we got that special gift from Santa, that our world would be perfect and that we would experience perfect and eternal happiness. Santa granted our wish, but by the time the twelfth day of Christmas rolled around, we were already bored with our special gift.

It is well documented that emotions, positive and negative, can affect our health. Our health can also affect our emotions. It is easier to be in a positive emotional state when our health is good, just as it requires more effort to maintain a positive state of mind when our health is poor. The interactions between our finances and our emotions are also well documented. Our finances can trigger some of our strongest emotions, and our emotions can trigger some of our worst financial decisions.

BECOMING WHEALTHY

Conventional wisdom in psychology is that we have two independent systems in our brain that are both working at all times. We can dub them the emotional side and the rational side. Psychologist Jonathan Haidt wrote in his book *The Happiness Hypothesis* that the emotional side is like an elephant and that the rational side is like the rider. The rider, by virtue of superior intelligence and a firm grasp of the reins, appears to be in control. As long as the elephant doesn't disagree with the rider, both move along smoothly in the same direction. However, whenever the six-ton elephant of your emotions decides to go in a direction with which your rational rider disagrees, your rational rider quickly finds out he/she is powerless to change direction.

Your wealth and your health, two attributes of great importance to you, are almost certainly less than they could be and probably less than they should be. Your rational rider wants to take only the path that leads to becoming whealthy. If you aren't there, it's because your emotional elephant takes too many detours and your rational rider can do very little to change course when that happens. Such a situation hardly makes you bad - it merely means you're human.

When we believe we are in greater control of our emotions than we really are, we are listening to our ego, which is one of the biggest single ingredients in the emotional elephant. Our ego has a hard time accepting that our rational goal of avoiding a heart attack can be sabotaged by the siren song of a Big Mac. Our ego has a hard time accepting that our rational goal of saving 10% of our income can be sabotaged by a penchant for fine footwear. No one wants to think their futures can be so compromised by such pedestrian temptations, but it happens every day to millions of people all over the world. Everyone spends every day wrestling with a six-ton elephant, and the elephant is going to win more than you want it to win. Now you know why you're so tired at the end of the day. Wrestling elephants is exhausting.

Our emotions aren't always our enemy, though. Our rational selves may be good at keeping us on the straight and narrow, but it takes our emotions (the good ones) to get us to move mountains.

Positive emotions are the greatest tools you will ever possess in your quest to become whealthy. If positive feelings like love, camaraderie, compassion, gratitude, mercy, and empathy can't get you moving in the right direction, you might as well be dead.

Haidt likes to use the analogy of the elephant and the rider to express the interaction between our emotional and rational sides. I like that analogy, but I want to use another one as well. I see the relationship between our emotional and rational sides the same way I see the relationship between a ship's sails and its rudder. A ship goes nowhere without its sails, but it can't go in the right direction without its rudder.

We can't go anywhere without the propulsion of emotion. We fill the sails of our emotions whenever we develop strong feelings for someone or something. Those sails can be filled from events like September 11 to the birth of your first grandchild to your favorite team making it to the finals. Positive emotions fill our sails in a way that requires minimal effort at the rudder, though the rudder must still be manned (womanned?).

Your rational rudder is useless on its own. It needs the movement generated by emotion to enable the rudder to have any purpose. The only way you can ever sail to your goal is to have both the sail and the rudder working toward that goal, to have both your rational side and your emotional side in sync in terms of wanting the same thing. When that happens, it's smooth sailing. When it doesn't happen, you can find yourself dead in the water and unable to move to safety when the seas get rough.

A rudder without sails is useless; sails without a rudder is dangerous. People who are logical, rational, and unemotional rarely cause harm, but they also don't do much to make the world a more pleasant place, either for others or for themselves. On the other hand, people who are illogical, irrational, and emotional may be exciting, but dangerous.

When it comes to the day-to-day, bad is stronger than good. We are better at labeling, recognizing, and feeling negative emotions than we are with positive ones. We spend more time on negative stories in the news than positive ones. We remember something bad that someone did more clearly and longer than something comparably good that the same person did. There seems to be a natural predilection to focus on negative emotions.

We may be genetically predisposed to focusing more on the negative than the positive. Conventional thinking is that having all positive emotions and always seeing the glass as half full leads to complacency, which is the first step to extinction. Negative emotions are evidence that you are aware of problems and are focused on finding solutions, which is an essential part of survival. Only when you see the glass as half empty are you likely to make any attempt to fill it all the way.

Negative emotions are useful when a problem needs a quick and specific solution. Showing pictures of starving children in a third world slum is an effective way of soliciting donations. Getting mad at yourself for making a mistake is likely to keep you from making the same mistake again soon. However, there is a natural tendency to seek quick and specific solutions to problems that require more nuanced and long-term answers.

Positive emotions are something of an enigma. In contrast to negative emotions, they are less likely to produce some specific action. When we're angry, we feel compelled to *do* something. When we're content, we are more likely to just bask for a while in the contentment. Negative emotions also have more signature facial expressions. It's easier to read a person's particular negative emotional state by his/her facial expression than it is to read the same person's positive emotional state in the same manner.

Negative emotions tend to narrow our thoughts, which is to be expected if negative emotions cause us to look for solutions to a problem. When we're in problem-solving mode, we get focused on solving the problem and tune out everything else. In contrast, positive emotions tend to broaden our thoughts and actions.

Work too often conjures up negative emotions. As a result, we become very focused and task-oriented when at work. We work on completing these tasks to complete our work and thereby free ourselves from these negative emotions. In contrast, when we play we don't follow a script, and we aren't thinking about completing any tasks. We are open to new ideas and new ways of doing things. It's not a coincidence that the companies that create an environment where work feels more like play generate more positive emotions from their workers, and those workers are also more creative in their work.

When we think of taking on a challenge like becoming whealthy, it is natural to think in terms of success and failure. Success and failure are not emotions; they are outcomes. Success and failure are also nouns; they are not adjectives. You may *have* a success or a failure; you *are not* a success or a failure.

Success and failure have an emotional connection because two of our most powerful emotions are linked closely to them - success with happiness and failure with sadness. We naturally assume that when we are successful at something, happiness will immediately ensue. We also expect failure to bring sadness.

Because it is easier to generate negative emotions than positive ones and because we expect to feel sad when we fail, our expectations of sadness are almost always met. Ironically, one of the keys to success is to not let failure sadden you to the point of becoming discouraged. People like Thomas Edison failed far more often than they succeeded, yet ultimately such people are hailed as being extremely successful.

Success generating happiness is a much trickier proposition. People equate success with happiness, and they often use the terms synonymously. Achieving success can often prove disappointing, though.

For example, a young woman may have a goal of reaching a certain management level at work. She may work long hours and make many sacrifices to climb the corporate ladder. Once the big promotion finally is received, she may experience more emptiness than elation. She may have the title, the salary, and the corner office. However, the rush of happiness she was expecting as part of the package isn't there because, contrary to popular expectations, happiness is not standard equipment on success. Also, because happiness did not come automatically, she can be left feeling not merely neutral but sad because her expectations were so unmet.

BECOMING WHEALTHY

Success and failure are travelling companions. As you journey toward a goal, you will inevitably encounter both along the way. Harvard business professor Rosabeth Moss Kanter, who has studied many business organizations, observed: "Everything can look like failure in the middle." If you understand that failures along the way are an inevitable part of long-term success and if that recognition enables you to control the negative emotions that come along with those failures, you are much more likely to persevere to the point of eventual success.

When we begin a new challenge, such as becoming whealthy, we start out with many positive emotions - hope being perhaps the strongest of them all. Hope is an essential emotion in getting any project off the ground, but as Sir Francis Bacon observed, "Hope is a good breakfast, but it is a poor supper." Once the initial excitement at the beginning of the journey has waned and the long slog toward the finish line is all there is at the moment, we can become like kids in the back seat on a long drive - "Are we there yet? Are we there yet? Are we there yet?"

When a goal becomes closer to realization, our emotions improve, with confidence of success leading the way. There is a U-shape to the emotional pattern we encounter when we work toward a long-term goal - hope and anticipation at the beginning, confidence and pride toward the end, but a cornucopia of negative emotions in the middle, including but not limited to, anger, cynicism, depression, despair, impatience, stress, and uncertainty.

The onset of negative emotions is much less likely to slow us down, and they are also likely to be fewer and of lower intensity if we anticipate their arrival and prepare accordingly.

Think about the pattern of going to college. At the beginning, you were full of hope and enthusiasm for this grand new experience you were about to have. Toward the end, you were focused on completing your degree with the pride and anticipation of becoming a college graduate. However, in between, there were three (or four or five) years of eight o'clock classes, boring lectures, ridiculously long term papers, and stressful weeks of final exams. When students fail to complete their degree, that failure is not usually because of a lack of intelligence or even discipline, but rather an inability to handle the march through the valley of negative emotions.

What these students experience in that middle period is *growth.* The growth mindset is simply acknowledging that there will be failures, setbacks, bad feelings, and the rest. The growth is in the acceptance of all the negatives and then rising above them, even getting psyched up at the challenge of conquering the drudgery that comes with any job.

Knowing that we will face valleys along the way to our goals can actually make us optimistic. Knowing that failure is going to cross our path on the journey to success, we are more likely to seek it out and confront it, rather than fearing and avoiding it. It isn't the obstacle that we choose to face head-on that defeats us; it's the object that blindsides us because we refuse to acknowledge it.

Positive emotions are a great asset in problem-solving, of which there is always a lot in the course of accomplishing a large goal. Doctors experiencing positive emotions can find solutions to medical dilemmas more readily. Students in a positive frame of mind devise more creative solutions to technical problems. Negotiators, who seek win-win solutions, reach such solutions far more quickly and easily when they are feeling positive in general and positive in particular about the outcome.

Whether you would be classified as an optimist or a pessimist may not be within your control as much as you would like. An optimistic attitude is largely inherited, though that doesn't mean you can't evolve from one to the other over time. The value of being an optimist has been articulated beautifully by Daniel Kahneman:

"If you were allowed one wish for your child, seriously consider wishing him or her optimism. Optimists are normally cheerful and happy, and therefore popular; they are resilient in adapting to failures and hardships, their chances of clinical depression are reduced, their immune system is stronger, they take better care of their health, they feel healthier than others and are in fact likely to live longer. Optimistic individuals play a disproportionate role in shaping our lives. Their decisions make a difference; they are the inventors, the entrepreneurs, the political and military leaders - not average people."

One of the keys to becoming whealthy is persistence, and two of the benefits of an optimistic temperament are persistence in the face of obstacles and resilience in the face of setbacks. If the first step in achieving a goal is the belief that you can and will achieve that goal, optimism is the first, most important tool to have in your kit.

Optimism can be viewed as a cornucopia of positive emotions molded into a single personality. Those positive emotions and optimism have a convoluted cause and effect pattern. When you possess positive emotions like confidence, enthusiasm, and inner peace, it's easy to be an optimist. Going the other way, if you are a natural optimist, positive emotions like confidence, enthusiasm, and inner peace seem to pour forth like a natural spring. Whether you are a natural-born optimist or have made yourself into one, once you are one, the positive emotions seem almost self-generating.

Optimism can be taken to the extreme, though. Daniel Kahneman also points out that the blessings of optimism are offered only to individuals who are only mildly biased and who are able to accentuate the positive without losing track of reality. The overly optimistic person is likely to take excessive risks. Many fortunes have been lost because people refused to accurately assess or even acknowledge the downside potential of an investment. Every economic bubble that bursts is testament to the dangers over over-optimism. It is important to believe that you can handle a worst-case scenario. In order for that belief to have value, you first have to be able to accurately gauge what the worst-case scenario actually is.

Negative emotions are ingrained in us as a necessary tool for survival. Imagine how long we would have survived as a species had we not been instilled with emotions like fear. However, it requires positive emotions like faith, hope, and love to take us beyond mere survival to personal growth and development. Even though positive emotions may not be with us all the time, when we experience them, we are more open to new relationships and experiences that benefit us in the long run. This openness not only allows us to absorb and create positive experiences more readily, it also enables us to better handle the setbacks and tragedies of life.

BECOMING WHEALTHY

Positive emotions, like gratitude, enable us, at times of loss, to feel appreciation for what we had, rather than feel resentment for what we lost.

Negative emotions have been proven to create physical stresses that are damaging to our health. Positive emotions have been proven to reduce the damage caused by negative emotions. Positive emotions also have a multiplier effect - feeling good now increases your chances of feeling good in the future. Experiencing positive emotions creates an upward spiral of continued growth and thriving.

Positive emotions benefit more than individuals. People who have positive emotions are more helpful to others. They are more selfless and more altruistic. They give more of their time, talent, and treasure to others. People who demonstrate positive emotions on a consistent basis help others to cultivate their own positive emotions. They are also more popular and more admired.

Think about the people with whom you most enjoy spending time and people you most admire and want to emulate. They are probably, without exception, people who demonstrate positive emotions on a consistent basis. If they have negative emotions, they try not to burden others with them.

Becoming whealthy is not something that happens overnight, or even in the short-term. It is something that develops slowly over months, years, and decades. Negative emotions that force you to look for short-term immediate fixes serve no purpose and are likely to be counterproductive in your desire to become whealthy.

People quickly tire of negative emotions, even their own. They never tire of positive ones. The aim of becoming whealthy is too broad and too deep to succeed

BECOMING WHEALTHY

without all the positive emotions you can muster. You might be able to cheer yourself to whealth; you won't be able to yell yourself there.

Becoming PHYSICALLY STRONGER

THE BUILDER OF A TEMPLE
by Henry David Thoreau

Every man is the builder of a temple,
Called his body,
To the God he worships,
After a style peculiarly his own,
Nor can he get off
By hammering marble instead.
We are all sculptors and painters,
And our material is
Our own flesh and blood.

Imagine you are given a new car at birth. Imagine also that this is the only car you will have for your entire lifetime. This car will have to fill all your transportation needs for seven, eight, or nine decades. It will be in constant use. Its condition and performance will have an enormous impact on your life, from your ability to attract mates to your ability to respond to crises.

Repairs can be made to your car, but they are almost always expensive. Parts are also in short supply, and many of the most critical parts, such as pistons or fuel injectors, may not even be available to fit your car. Replacement parts also have no warranty and rarely work as well as the original equipment.

Major damage to your car may also be irreparable. If too many parts are damaged, either through an accident, abuse, or merely through neglect, the vehicle may have to be totaled. In such a case, you do not get a replacement vehicle. You never get a replacement vehicle. This one car is the only car you're allowed to own for your entire lifetime.

If you had just one car to last a lifetime, how would you care for it? Would you make sure that all - and I mean all - of the routine maintenance was done correctly and on schedule? Would you make sure that the car was washed and waxed to protect the exterior? Would you make sure the interior was kept clean and protected from damage and deterioration, too? Would you be very careful when driving the car, to make sure you or others did not inflict irreparable damage to the car? Would you insist that any passengers treat your car with the proper respect? Would you ever loan the car to someone, knowing the risks if they damaged it beyond repair?

The idea of having only one car to last a lifetime seems rather preposterous to us. We actually have a very similar situation, only it isn't merely a car. The repercussions of inadequate care are far greater, too.

At birth we are each issued one body, and that body must last us our entire lifetime. Both the quality and quantity of that lifetime depend a great deal on the quality of care we give to our body during that lifetime. Repairs are very expensive. Replacement parts, such as organs, are sometimes unattainable, and they come with no warranty and rarely work as well as the original equipment. Major damage, whether through accident, abuse, or mere neglect, may be impossible to repair, resulting in the end of your life, or at least the end of your life as you wanted to live it.

Many people actually take better care of their cars than they do their bodies. They perform the routine maintenance on the car, but they fail to get routine physicals. They protect their cars with a coat of wax, but they don't use sunscreen. They are quick to attend to a minor malfunction on the car before it becomes a major one, but they ignore their body's signs of a malfunction until it is impossible to ignore, or until it leads to a full-blown breakdown.

It can't be the cost difference between repairing a car and repairing a body that leads to this disparity in care. The cost of a minor operation can equal or exceed the total cost of a new car. It can't be the need to impress others that leads to disparity. In general, people are more impressed with those who take care of their physical appearance and neglect their cars than they are with those who take care of their cars and neglect their physical appearance. It can't be the greater utility of one's car over one's body that leads to disparity. People around the world today and throughout history have gotten along fine without cars; no one gets along without a body.

In short, everything we hope to accomplish during our lifetime depends a great deal on how well we take care of our bodies, the original one-to-a-customer giveaway. If you take care of your body, you will greatly increase your chances of success in almost every single endeavor. If you neglect, mismanage, or abuse your body, you will severely compromise your level of performance in almost anything you attempt in your lifetime.

Why do we, as a population, take rather poor care of our bodies, at least in comparison to the care we give to our other possessions? There are two general reasons for this tendency to take our bodies and our health for granted. First, almost all the things we do to hurt our health are really enjoyable when we're doing them - overeating, taking drugs, having unprotected sex - it's a very long list. Second, the human body has evolved over hundreds of thousands of years to repair itself quite effectively. It takes a serious attack on the body to put a human out of commission permanently. Our bodies also don't discriminate between damage caused by external forces and that caused by our own actions. Our bodies will keep trying to make repairs up to the point that making the repairs actually harms the body by allocating resources to a suboptimal use. The body's dedication to its health and preservation is often underappreciated by its owner, which can lead the owner to shirk his/her responsibilities in keeping everything in good working order.

Even when the body is unable to totally repair damage that it has incurred, we can be confident that there are external cures. In 2015, there were enough prescriptions filled for a dozen prescriptions for every man, woman, and child in the U.S. The population of the U.S. is about 4% of the world total, yet we consume nearly 50% of the world's prescription drugs. The average American takes 20 to 25 times as many prescription drugs as the average non-American.

One reason for the overuse of prescription drugs is that taking drugs is a path of least resistance. To the overworked and time-stressed physician, writing a prescription is a way of treating the symptoms of a patient's problem, which is quicker and easier than tracking down the root causes. Discovering the root causes of health issues does not mean there is an easy cure.

The patient defers to the physician's greater wisdom when it comes to health care. If the doctor thinks a prescription is the best way to treat a problem, few patients will ask about alternatives. Taking a pill also requires no effort on the part of the patient. Given the choice of treating a symptom with no effort or treating a cause with considerable effort, most people opt for the former.

Accidental deaths caused by medication overdoses now exceed deaths from car crashes, making it the leading cause of accidental deaths in the U.S. Ten percent of Americans are on a daily regimen of some kind of anti-depressant medication. Because the pace of life increases far faster than our ability to evolve to handle it, drugs are one way many people cope with the unique stresses of life in the 21st century. However, when you look at people who seem to do best at handling the stresses of modern life, they tend to be those who focus on maintaining a healthy body, mind, and soul. These people supplement the body's biological immune system by developing a psychological immune system to handle the new threats to our well-being.

Perhaps the largest single cause of stress in people's lives today is the feeling that we do not have enough time. Entire books have been written on how to better manage your time, though taking the time to read an entire book on time management may not be good time management itself. If time is money, then many of the principles that apply to money management can also be applied to time management. Perhaps the best money management rule to apply to time management is "pay yourself first."

In money management, pay yourself first refers to putting money aside that will benefit and support you in the long term before allocating money to anything else. You pay yourself first when you have money deducted from your paycheck to go into your retirement fund at work.

Paying yourself first with your time is about setting aside specific blocks of time each day to do the things that are necessary to keep you going in the long run - time to sleep, time to exercise, time to socialize, time for solitude. Time allocated for these essential activities should be sacred. These blocks of time are the top priorities, and mundane tasks, petty annoyances, and inconsiderate others should not be allowed to invade these periods.

Of course, no one is going to respect these inviolable periods unless you respect them first. Once you establish a regular schedule for sleep, exercise, socializing, and solitude *and once you refuse to let yourself violate those periods*, people will recognize and respect your priorities. By setting these boundaries that may not be crossed, you are not telling others "no"; you are telling them "not now." If someone is unwilling to respect your position, it may be time to question if they are worth *any* of your time. Remember, any organism that does not set aside time for regeneration is eventually consumed.

Even when you set aside sufficient blocks of time for sleep, exercise, socializing, and solitude, you have a lot of time still to be managed. There are tasks and responsibilities that have to be executed every day, and the best way to make sure that the most gets done is to prioritize what merits your attention. Setting priorities may be as simple as making a list at the beginning of the week of the important things that have to be done that week, and then knocking out the most pressing and the most unpleasant tasks first. Some tasks don't provide a lot of leeway as to when they get done, but proper time management can at least assure that those tasks don't intrude into the sacred periods.

BECOMING WHEALTHY

Unfinished business is a major stress inducer, which is one reason why so many people feel compelled to have to do everything at once. Making a list actually helps reduce the pressure of unfinished business because the list will remind you of what needs to be done without being obnoxious about it. When you know that you won't forget an important task and that you've set it up to be taken care of, you can then forget about it and focus on the task you're doing now, which enables you to do that task more efficiently and effectively.

Procrastinators are notoriously poor at time management. As a result, they get stressed out because they let things pile up to the point they become overwhelming. Prioritizing helps you identify what tasks can wait until tomorrow, next week, or even next year - it isn't procrastination; it's prioritization.

We all admire the Good Samaritan. Most of us try to emulate the Samaritan's kindness whenever possible. There's an interesting aspect to that story that is too often overlooked, though. After the Samaritan made sure the robbery victim was in good hands, he told the innkeeper that he would settle up any additional expenses upon his return, and then he went on his way. The Samaritan had business to attend to, and if he didn't take care of that business, he wouldn't have been in a position to provide assistance the next time it was needed. The Good Samaritan is not just a parable about helping others; it's a parable about having your priorities right. It's about making sure to take care of yourself so that you can be in the best position to help the most people for the longest time. It's about priorities, pacing, and preservation. These are the purposes of time management, and time management is stress management.

After time management issues, another great cause of stress is our inability to distinguish between what we can control and what we cannot. Not taking control when we can and should take control can lead to victimization, or at least to a victim mentality. Trying to take control of things that are beyond our control can lead to the kind of stress that can result in a premature trip to the ER, or the morgue.

As stated previously, we have the ability to control our input to a situation, but often the eventual outcome is beyond our control. Jawaharlal Nehru, the first Prime Minister of India, said, "Life is like a game of cards. The hand that is dealt you represents determinism; the way you play it is free will."

Recognizing that we can control our inputs, but not necessarily control outcomes, can take a lot of the stress out of situations. If we focus on inputs instead of outcomes, not only will our stress levels drop, but the outcomes themselves are likely to be better, too.

Unless someone is gaming the system, outcomes are inexorably linked to inputs. By focusing on what we can control (inputs), we actually gain more control over what we can't control directly (outcomes).

We can also add unnecessary stress to our lives when we overestimate the effect certain outcomes are likely to have on our lives. This phenomenon is particularly noticeable in two areas - sports and elections.

While it's great to enjoy sports and root for the home team, when we let too much of our identity and reason for living get tied up with things beyond our control, we invite unnecessary stress and frustration into our lives. When you consider that there can be only one champion, it's highly likely your team will provide more frustration than elation.

Elections certainly do impact people's lives, and we all have a duty to participate in the democratic process. However, it's important to stop and think about how much in your daily life actually changes when, for example, the resident in the White House changes. How elections affect us is largely the result of how much we *allow* the results to affect us.

"God, grant me the serenity to accept the things I cannot change, the courage to change the things I can, and the wisdom to know the difference." The opposite of stress is serenity. The serenity prayer is so widely utilized because it first encourages us to accept what we cannot change, and what we cannot change most often in life are outcomes. Serenity is the product of accepting that some things are beyond our control.

Nearly three thousand years ago, there lived in China a saint named Budai. He would go from village to village, stand near a square or a corner and laugh full-heartedly and freely. Not stopping to talk with anyone, he would go on laughing. People would gather together, and, seeing that Budai was laughing, they would begin to laugh loudly, too. Wherever Budai went, the health of the people began to improve. People of many villages regarded Budai as a Divine Being and named him Laughing Buddha.

Laughter is the best medicine, and it is one of the greatest stress relievers ever created. In the short term, laughter increases your intake of oxygen; stimulates your heart, lungs, and muscles; and increases the supply of those wonderful endorphins to your brain. The long term benefits of laughter are even more impressive.

The positive thoughts triggered by laughter release neuropeptides that help fight stress and potentially more serious illnesses. Laughter also reduces pain by producing natural painkillers in the body, such as the antibody IGA. Laughter can actually provide a workout, too. Researchers estimate that laughing 100 times is equal to 10 minutes on a rowing machine or 15 minutes on an exercise bike. Laughter also exercises your abdominal, respiratory, facial, leg, and back muscles. If you've ever felt winded after an intense bout of laughter, it's because you've just had a pretty intense workout.

Dr. Mike Evans is an Associate Professor of Family Medicine and Public Health at the University of Toronto and a staff physician at St. Michael's Hospital. His research has led him to discover a treatment that has remarkable curative powers. The research has proven that this treatment has:

- Reduced pain resulting from knee surgeries by 47%
- Reduced levels of dementia and Alzheimer's disease by 50%
- Reduced the progression rate of diabetes by 58%
- Reduced risk of hip fractures in elderly women by 41%
- Reduced anxiety levels by 48%
- Reduced depression in over 40% of cases
- Improved overall quality of life more than any other treatment.

You've heard of this miracle treatment, and you may even be taking it today. It's called exercise.

You shouldn't be disappointed to find out that the most successful method of retaining and regaining health and strength is something as basic as exercise. Exercise is free; it's available to everyone who can move, and it can do more to help people handle the rigors of their lives than anything that could ever come out of a laboratory. If we're disappointed that the miracle cure is exercise, it's because we know that we will have to make an effort beyond swallowing a pill to make this miracle treatment work for us.

The Mayo Clinic cites seven key benefits to exercise:
- Exercise controls weight.
- Exercise combats health conditions and diseases
- Exercise improves mood.
- Exercise boosts energy.
- Exercise promotes better sleep.
- Exercise improves your sex life.

The benefits cited by the Mayo Clinic are just the tip of the benefits iceberg. Harvard Medical School psychiatrist John Ratey notes that exercise is the single best thing you can do for your brain in terms of memory, mood, and learning. Exercise reverses the detrimental effects of stress by releasing soothing chemicals in the brain like serotonin, dopamine, and norepinephrine. A study done at UC-San Francisco showed that exercise may actually work on a cellular level to reverse stress's toll on the aging process.

Burning off 350 calories three times a week through sustained, sweat-inducing activity has been shown in many cases to reduce symptoms of depression as effectively as anti-depressants. The exercise appears to stimulate neuron growth in areas of the brain damaged by depression. Exercises like yoga can be used to complement, but not substitute, drug treatment for depression.

Exercise increases brain chemicals known as growth factors, which help make new brain cells and establish new connections between brain cells that facilitate learning. Complicated physical activities, such as playing tennis or dancing, provide the biggest brain boost.

Exercise improves self-esteem and improves body image. These improvements can come from liking the results you get from exercise when you get on a scale or look in the mirror. There is also the boost to self-esteem when you find you can run faster or farther than you could six months ago.

Moderate physical activities like walking have been proven to greatly reduce the decline of memory function in the elderly. Being sedentary is bad at any age, but its effects, especially on the brain, are more telling and more intense for those over age 70. Until a drug is invented that can cure Alzheimer's disease, the next best thing is to be physically and mentally stimulated through activity.

So how much exercise does it take to reap the kinds of benefits that are listed? Dr. Evans believes that 30 minutes a day of moderate exercise can achieve most of the results the average person is seeking. Because people have a natural disinclination to commit to 30 minutes of exercise a day, Dr. Evans asks instead if you are willing to limit the sedentary part of your day to 23½ hours. Put into that context, moving around for $1/48^{th}$ of the day doesn't seem so hard.

No one goes from being a couch potato to training for the Iron Man Triathlon in one fell swoop. The first step is to get off the couch and walk around the neighborhood for 30 minutes in the evening and develop that into a daily habit. The benefits from that activity will soon become evident, and the walk may increase in length or develop a faster pace. Other exercises may creep into the daily routine, such as yoga or lifting weights, as your energy level increases.

Over a period of time, say a year, the metamorphosis becomes undeniable to everyone. At that point, the individual has not only changed physically, but mentally as well. It is at this stage that a person begins to realize his/her still untapped potential and begins looking for a new challenge.

Because our brain is still the same basic brain that our ancestors had a few hundred thousand years ago, it is still designed to look for ways to do as little work as possible. This design feature was very useful until just a few decades ago. Until the internal combustion engine became commonplace, almost everyone walked at least 30 minutes a day, whether they wanted to or not. We also had to lug and lift, push and pull, so a typical day for the typical human included more than enough aerobic and strength training to last a modern person a week.

It is estimated that we would have to add a 12-mile walk to our daily routines to equal the energy output of our ancestors. Those ancestors were also estimated to consume only about 400 more calories per day than modern humans. If the average person takes 3 to 4 miles of walking to burn 400 calories, the reason we are fat and that they weren't is because they walked the equivalent of 8 more miles every day than we do while consuming the same amount of calories.

When you do aerobic exercise where you raise your heart rate and sustain it (such as jogging or swimming), you are enabling your body to generate greater amounts of horsepower. One horsepower equals 33,000 ft.lbs. per minute. One way to calculate your personal horsepower is to figure out how many feet you can run in one minute. Multiply that distance in feet times your weight in pounds. That total, divided by 33,000, tells you how many horsepower you generate.

For example, if a person weighs 165 pounds and can cover 800 feet in a minute, that person generates exactly 4 horsepower [(165 x 800)/33,000 = 4.0]. Generating higher horsepower, as well as generating lower times, can be a motivator to run faster.

Torque measures the ability to move an object around an axis, fulcrum, or pivot. When you do strength training, such as lifting weights, you are enabling your body to generate greater amounts of torque. Every time you lift a weight, you are moving an object around an axis, typically a body joint. The more weight you move, the more torque is required. Just as an engine must generate both horsepower and torque to do its job, our bodies need aerobic exercise and strength training to enable us to do our jobs.

There is an almost endless variety of physical activities that constitute exercise, so everyone should be able to find some form of activity that is enjoyable. Remember what Mark Twain professed - work is what you have to do, and play is what you want to do. The best way to get into a habit of regular exercise is to find something that feels like play and also gets you moving.

Children who get sufficient exercise do not go out for a jog or hit the weight room. They get their exercise by accident, through play that has them running, jumping, swimming, etc. Adults who play games, such as tennis, know they are getting beneficial exercise, but the main reason they play tennis is they like playing tennis.

Playing games as exercise also has a social component. Tennis players enjoy the game and benefit from the exercise, but they also enjoy sharing the activity with others. The social aspect can be an additional incentive to take part in a physical activity even when your body might not be quite feeling up to it.

Activities that involve others can also provide motivation because we don't want to let others down by our absence. Team sports are especially good at keeping us from skipping out just because we aren't in the mood that day.

The best activities to use as exercise are ones that you would enjoy doing even if the benefits of exercise were absent. If you've ever seen a group of seniors in a bowling league, they always seem to be having a great time. They would want to keep bowling even if they weren't getting exercise. They will keep showing up to bowl until they are no longer able.

Here is a list of activities that qualify as exercise that people actually like to do. All you have to do is find one or two you like and go at it:

Aerobics, ballet, baseball, basketball, biking, boating, bowling, boxing, canoeing, dance revolution, dancing, field hockey, football, Frisbee, golf, gymnastics, hiking, hockey, hopscotch, horseback riding, hula hooping, ice skating, jogging, juggling, jump rope, lacrosse, laser tag, paintball, ping-pong, playing catch, rock climbing, roller blading, roller skating, running, skateboarding, skiing, soccer, softball, swimming, tae kwon do, tennis, trampoline, treadmill, unicycling, volleyball, walking, weightlifting, Wii sports games.

Employers who enable workers to exercise during work hours have found they have healthier, more productive workers. A study at the University of Bristol in the U.K. showed that after exercising, participants returned to work more tolerant of themselves and more forgiving of their colleagues. Their work performance was also consistently higher, based on several measures. Employers who sacrifice some work time for employee exercise more than make up the difference in increased productivity, fewer sick days, and improved cooperation among employees.

Speaking of productivity, few things impede a person's productivity, not to mention damaging health, like an insufficient amount of sleep. There are two kinds of sleep deprivation. Acute sleep deprivation is when you go for days without sleep. Acute sleep deprivation has major effects on the mind and body and is classified as torture by Amnesty international. However, the body is able to recover from acute sleep deprivation in a matter of days in most cases. The much larger and more serious problem is chronic sleep deprivation.

Sleep studies that have been conducted where subjects are put into environments with no clocks and windows and are instructed to sleep whenever they feel tired have shown that 95% sleep between 7 and 8 hours a night. Only 2.5% sleep more than 8 hours and only 2.5% intentionally sleep less. While adults need 7 to 8 hours of sleep, adolescents (10-17 years) need 8.5 to 9.5 hours; school age children (5-10 years) need 10 to 11 hours, and preschoolers need 11 to 13 hours of sleep every 24 hours.

As modern life makes more demands on our time, exercise is one use of time that gets short-changed. However, many people get enough exercise in their daily activity, and many people don't exercise even when time is plentiful. Everyone sleeps, to a greater or lesser degree, and because sleep consumes a good chunk of the 24-hour cycle, it is the first area to surrender time when it is needed for more "urgent" matters.

If you have chronic sleep deprivation, you may suffer some of these short-term consequences:
- Sleep deprivation induces significant reductions in performance and alertness. Reducing your nighttime

sleep by as little as one-and-a-half hours for just one night could result in a reduction of daytime alertness by as much as 32%.
- Decreased alertness and excessive daytime sleepiness impair your memory and your cognitive ability - your ability to think and process information.
- Disruption of a bed partner's sleep due to a sleep disorder may cause significant problems for the relationship (for example, separate bedrooms, conflicts, moodiness, etc.).
- You may experience a poor quality of life. For example, you might be unable to participate in certain activities that require sustained attention, like going to the movies, seeing your child in a school play, or watching a favorite TV show.
- Excessive sleepiness also contributes to a greater than two-fold higher risk of sustaining an occupational injury.
- The National Highway Traffic Safety Administration (NHTSA) estimates conservatively that each year drowsy driving is responsible for at least 100,000 automobile crashes, 71,000 injuries, and 1,550 fatalities.

As unpleasant as these consequences are, the long-term consequences of chronic sleep deprivation are worse and include:
- High blood pressure
- Heart attack
- Heart failure
- Stroke
- Obesity
- Depression and other mood disorders
- Mental impairment

- Fetal and childhood growth retardation

One of the reasons so many of us deprive ourselves of sleep is the misguided notion that sleep is unproductive time and that an hour spent working instead of sleeping is a better use of our time. Research has consistently shown that sacrificing one hour of needed sleep reduces productivity the following day by much more than one hour. Sleep denied also has a steep curve of diminishing returns. Thirty minutes of foregone sleep might cost you thirty minutes of productivity; sixty minutes might cost you ninety minutes; two hours of lost sleep can cut your productivity in half the following day.

The Harvard Women's Health Watch suggests six reasons to get enough sleep:

1. **Learning and memory**: Sleep helps the brain commit new information to memory through a process called memory consolidation. In studies, people who'd slept after learning a task did better on tests later.
2. **Metabolism and weight**: Chronic sleep deprivation may cause weight gain by affecting the way our bodies process and store carbohydrates and by altering levels of hormones that affect our appetite.
3. **Safety**: Sleep debt contributes to a greater tendency to fall asleep during the daytime. These lapses may cause falls and mistakes such as medical errors, air traffic mishaps, and road accidents.
4. **Mood**: Sleep loss may result in irritability, impatience, inability to concentrate, and moodiness. Too little sleep can also leave you too tired to do the things you like to do.

5. **Cardiovascular health**: Serious sleep disorders have been linked to hypertension, increased stress hormone levels, and irregular heartbeat.
6. **Disease**: Sleep deprivation alters immune function, including the activity of the body's killer cells. Keeping up with sleep may also help fight cancer.

Stress is the number one cause of short-term sleeping difficulties. Chronic stress can lead to chronic sleep disorders. Irregular schedules make it harder to develop a regular sleep habit, which is very important in maintaining a proper sleep schedule. Even changing sleep schedules on the weekend can cause sleep problems during the week. Going to sleep and waking up at about the same time every day is one of the best ways to get enough restful sleep.

According to leading sleep researchers, some of the best techniques to combat common sleep problems include:
- Keep a regular sleep/wake schedule.
- Keep caffeine use to a minimum, and take no caffeine 4 to 6 hours before bedtime.
- Don't smoke, especially near bedtime or if you awaken during the night.
- Avoid alcohol and heavy meals before sleep.
- Get regular exercise.
- Minimize noise, light, and temperature extremes in the bedroom.
- Try to awaken without an alarm clock.
- Try moving bedtime a little earlier every night for a period.

Chronic sleep deprivation can lead to irregular eating habits and overeating, which can lead to obesity and an entirely new set of health problems. Hunger can indicate a lack of proper rest if you are not very hungry when you first get up in the morning or if you are very hungry when you get home in the evening. Proper sleep can shift your eating from evening to morning, when the calories are both needed and less likely to turn into fat.

Problem-solving ability is directly linked to the quantity and quality of our sleep. Since more and more of our work requires us to use our problem-solving skills, chronic sleep deprivation can have a major impact on our ability to get the job done. Not only does sleep improve our ability to solve problems when we're awake, sleep itself is also a fertile field for creativity and problem solving.

Harvard psychologist Deidre Barrett tells us, "Dreams are just thinking in a different biochemical state. In the sleep state, the brain thinks much more visually and intuitively." This creative dream state is where a 22-year-old Paul McCartney came up with the melody for the most recorded song in history, *Yesterday*.

When we're working our brains to the white meat trying to solve a problem, sometimes the best solution is to "sleep on it." During sleep, the prefrontal cortex, the part of the brain that keeps your life in order, shuts down, leaving the brain to reassemble thoughts in ways that can make for some very strange dreams. That random disassembly and reassembly also enables pieces to come together in patterns that would never do so in conscious thought, much like the pieces that were assembled to create *Frankenstein*, the idea of which came to author Mary Shelley in a dream.

Sleep is to your health as "pay yourself first" is to your wealth. If you leave it to last, it never gets its proper share. When you pay yourself first by putting money into savings before paying anything else, you are not being selfish. You are making sure that you will be able to remain self-sufficient in the future. When you decline to do something, especially something to benefit others, because you need to get a decent night's sleep, you are also not being selfish. After a night of proper rest, you can then take care of those pending tasks, and you will be able to do them faster and better and with a more positive attitude than you ever could when you were sleep deprived.

Nearly a century ago, Roscoe "Fatty" Arbuckle was the biggest star in Hollywood. In 1914, Paramount Pictures was paying him $1,000 a day plus 25% of the profits. Arbuckle was big in another way, too. He was 5'10' and weighed an average of 260 pounds. At the time of his fame, the average adult American male weighed 135 pounds.

Today the average American male weighs just under 190 pounds, although we are about an inch taller than we were a century ago. You also wouldn't have to look very far today to find several men who are roughly the same weight as Fatty Arbuckle, though none of them could do the kinds of stunts Arbuckle could. The physical oddity of a century ago has become the norm of today.

Today, one in three Americans is classified as normal weight; one in three is classified as overweight; the final one in three is classified as obese. Obesity is defined as a medical condition in which body fat has accumulated to the extent that it may have an adverse effect on health, leading to shorter life expectancy and increased health problems. People are classified as obese when their body mass index (BMI) exceeds 30.

The obesity trend is also not expected to improve any time soon. Federal health officials predict that the national obesity rate will increase from its current level of 36% of the population to 42% by 2030. The trend cuts across all age groups, as baby boomers will become even more sedentary in retirement, sedentary children will grow into sedentary adults with even fewer external controls on their diet, and more and more overweight people slowly gain weight and cross the 30 BMI threshold into obesity.

Weight gain and loss are a simple function of arithmetic. If you consume more calories than you burn, you will gain weight. If you burn more calories than you consume, you will lose weight. Adjusting either variable will work. Adjusting both is almost always the safest and most effective way to lose weight. In order to lose one pound, the average person must burn 3500 more calories than consumed. Conversely, you gain a pound when the calories consumed exceed the calories burned by 3500.

Because people tend to underestimate the calories they consume and overestimate the calories the burn, they end up gaining weight without understanding how it happened. For example, wouldn't you feel entitled to a Snickers bar after a brisk 30-minute walk? Most people would say yes, but you would need to *jog* for 32 minutes or walk for *78* minutes to burn the 280 calories in a Snickers bar.

The number of calories each of us needs each day varies by our size, age, weight, gender, and activity level. A 120-pound, 80-year-old woman who is not active needs only about 1000 calories a day. A 200-pound, 30-year-old man who is physically active in his job and exercises daily needs at least 3500 calories a day. Of course, these figures are to maintain the stated weight. What does someone need to do to lose weight?

If 30 pounds of excess weight took 30 years to accumulate, why do people think they can shed it all in

1/60th of that time? Crash diets never work, and you can blame our ancestors. The human body has evolved over thousands of years to be very sensitive to drastic reductions in calorie intake.

When the calorie intake suddenly drops 50%, the body reads this as *famine*, and it does two things. It slows down the metabolism to maintain weight. Then, when calorie intake increases, the first thing the body does is store as many calories as possible as fat to provide insurance against the next famine. This act of preservation by the human body is why you end up fatter after a crash diet and why it's a terrible idea to try to do too much too fast.

Patience is a virtue, and patience and persistence are the only way to get weight off and keep it off. The way to successfully lose weight is not to attack the problem, but to ease up on it and slowly turn it in the right direction. Because large drops in calorie intake do more harm than good in the long run, it is necessary and far healthier to lose weight through a combination of lower calorie intake and greater calorie burn and to maintain both indefinitely.

One of the best ways to burn calories is walking, and there are several reasons. Walking is what humans do better than any other species. Our whole physical evolution is based on getting up on our back legs and strutting our stuff. You may not have been born to run, but you were definitely born to walk. Walking can be done anywhere, anytime, by anyone. It is low impact; it exercises the entire body as well as the cardiovascular system; it can be done alone or with others; it requires only shoes, but not always.

As a nation, we didn't get fat overnight, and we shouldn't try to get thin overnight, either. Common sense and moderation are the keys to success in both health and wealth. We don't need complex diets, complex equipment, or complexes of inferiority to get us from where we are healthwise to where we want and need to be.

If we do a little more, eat a little less, and simply keep doing it, we will add both quantity and quality to our lives, as well as saving hundreds of billions of dollars on medical care that we won't need.

Becoming FISCALLY STRONGER

SMART by Shel Silverstein

My dad gave me one dollar bill
'Cause I'm his smartest son,
And I swapped it for two shiny quarters
'Cause two is more than one!

And then I took the quarters
And traded them to Lou
For three dimes -- I guess he don't know
That three is more than two!

Just then, along came old blind Bates
And just 'cause he can't see
He gave me four nickels for my three dimes,
And four is more than three!

And I took the nickels to Hiram Coombs
Down at the seed-feed store,
And the fool gave me five pennies for them,
And five is more than four!

And then I went and showed my dad,
And he got red in the cheeks
And closed his eyes and shook his head--
Too proud of me to speak!

A few years ago, 470,000 15-year-old students from 34 industrialized countries took a math test. U.S. students participated in the test, as did students from countries like China, South Korea, Finland, Germany, and Canada. The math test had a maximum score of

1,000. The average score for all students was 496; the U.S. average score was 487, ranking us 25th out of the 34 industrialized nations that participated.

The reporting of these test results is not meant as an indictment of the U.S. education system, though these results would indicate there is a lot of work to be done in math classrooms across the country. The rankings of performance by country on the math test coincide closely with those countries' overall financial strength and stability.

If you're no good at math, there's a good chance you'll be no good with money, either. You can end up like the "smart" son in the poem, cleverly turning one dollar into five pennies.

What do you think of when you think of money? Everyone has a slightly different concept of money, but most people picture bills of various denominations when they think of money. Most people equate *money* with *currency*. We measure money with currency, but money itself is a measure of something very different - *purchasing power*.

In order to entice you to save and invest money, rather than spend it right away, banks, corporations, governments, and other institutions that want to use your money have to make it more appealing for you to give it to them than to spend it now. They entice you by offering to give you more money in the future than you give them in the present. Whether it's called interest or profit, the concept is the same - you will be rewarded with more money later if you don't spend it now.

Where finance gets complicated is when we have to calculate how much more money it will take to motivate us to delay gratification now for something better later. For prolific savers, it might not take much inducement in the form of interest rates to convince them to save, rather than spend. For prolific spenders, there may not be an interest rate high enough to induce them to delay gratification. Think back to the children in the Marshmallow test. They were offered the chance to receive twice as many marshmallows if they could delay gratification for 15 minutes, but only 1 in 3 could hold out.

Because money is, at its core, a measure of purchasing power, it is necessary to look at what a certain amount of money can buy now, compared to what it will buy in the future, to determine what kind of return is necessary to merit saving rather than spending. We are talking now about the connection between interest rates and inflation. When inflation is low, interest rates can be low; conversely, when inflation is high, interest rates must also be high to induce people to save, rather than spend.

Let's use a simple example to illustrate. You have $100 that you can either spend now or save for a year. You will receive a 5% interest rate; in a year you will receive $105. Inflation is 2%; everything that you could have bought for $100 now will cost $102 in a year. You may well decide it's worth it to save to get the increase in purchasing power in a year. On the other hand, the increase may not be sufficient to induce you to delay gratification. The human part of the equation is always the most unpredictable.

Let's make one change to the previous example. Everything you could have bought for $100 now will cost $107 in a year because inflation is 7%, not 2%. Even though the *currency* you receive after a year of saving will have increased, its *purchasing power* will actually be less.

Under these circumstances, you are penalized twice for saving. First, you don't get to enjoy what the money might have purchased for a whole year. Second, when you finally do get to buy something, you will get less of it than you would have a year earlier. The only way it makes sense to save in this and in any case is to get a return that increases your purchasing power compared to what it is now.

When we are going through uncertain economic times, people look for "safe" places to put their money. By safe, they think in terms of return of their currency. In many cases, though, they may be engaging in the very unsafe practice of losing purchasing power.

A bank may offer a one-year CD with an interest rate of 1% (while inflation is averaging 3%), and people will buy it because they feel that at least the money is earning *something*. However, in a year, everything will have increased in price by 3%, so they are assured of losing money, as measured by the only correct measure, purchasing power.

Whenever we try to plan for the future, there is always a large element of uncertainty involved. When we try to decide whether it's better to buy something now or to wait, we have to deal with the uncertainty of future prices, as well as the uncertainty of our financial needs in the future. Even if today might be the best time to buy something, we also have to consider our cash needs in the future. A lack of cash when we need it in the future may create an expense that wipes out any gain that might have been made by making a timely purchase in the present.

When we are uncertain, our tendency is to do nothing and wait. When economic patterns are uncertain, both individuals and corporations delay purchases and accumulate cash. While having a cash reserve is always a prudent part of any financial plan, becoming stagnant for fear of the unknown stifles progress.

Everyone looks to invest their money in something that is low risk and high return. There is only one problem with looking for such an investment - it doesn't exist. If there is one immutable law regarding finance it is this: risk and return move together. If you want a higher return on your investment, you have to be willing to accept more risk. If you are only willing to accept a low risk on your investment, you must also accept a low return. Any investment that claims to offer both high returns and low risk is a fraud.

The risk-reward connection is not hard to understand if you look at it from your personal perspective. If you make a bet on a coin toss, the odds are 1:1 that you will succeed, but the potential gain is equal to the potential loss. If you buy a Power Ball lottery ticket, the bet is high risk, as the odds are something on the order of 195 million to 1. You would never accept those odds to merely double what you paid for the ticket. In order to induce you to take such a high risk bet, the reward has to be sufficient. In the case of Power Ball jackpots, it's on the order of tens of millions of dollars. If the risk of losing is greater, the rewards must be greater, too.

Most of the millionaires in the United States are first generation wealthy, and their wealth is most often the result of creating a successful business. Most of us would love to be millionaires, and most of us would enjoy the prospect of running our own successful business. What keeps most of us from doing so is the risk that comes along with such a proposition.

Some 85% of businesses fail within the first three years. Even those that succeed had no guarantee of success when they started. Most had periods of great uncertainty along the way. When we see a successful, wealthy business owner, we see only the rewards. Seeing only the rewards can have two negative effects. It can blind us to the potential risks, which may cause us to make a reckless foray into a business of our own. Second, seeing only the rewards can create envy and distort our perception of what that successful business owner actually risked and sacrificed to achieve the success we wish we could have.

We all have different personality traits, including our individual tolerances for risk. It's important to remember the cause-effect relationship with your personal risk tolerance level. The reward you receive is determined by your risk tolerance; your risk tolerance is not determined by the reward you seek. If you have a low tolerance for risk, you will only hurt yourself if you go way outside your comfort zone to increase your potential reward.

If you start a business and the risk proves overwhelming, the business will fail, and you might wreck your health trying to make it succeed. If you make riskier investments than you can stomach for the chance of a bigger payoff, you will likely panic at the worst time and lose far more than you gain. You may also spend a lot of sleepless nights fretting over what can and is going wrong.

Although we all have a certain inborn risk tolerance, we can tweak that level through education. Madam Curie said, "Nothing is to be feared - it is only to be understood." We fear uncertainty, and much of our uncertainty is based on a lack of understanding of circumstances. People who have an initial fear of investing in stocks can often reduce that fear by learning what stocks actually are (ownership in the corporation), by understanding how stock prices are determined, and by understanding that short-term volatility does not impact long-term returns. A low risk tolerance based on a lack of understanding can be rectified, and it needs to be in order to enable someone to gain a fair share of the rewards.

There are two emotions that, above all others, are likely to wreak immeasurable damage to a person's financial health. These two emotions are greed and fear.

Greed causes us to place too great a value on the things that money can buy and too little value on the things that money can't buy. We pay the price of greed in a loss of our humanity, as we focus more on things than people. Fear - the kind that comes from thinking too much - can paralyze us when the situation demands action. Fear leads us to trade long-term suffering for short-term comfort.

There is a formula to keep greed and fear from ever gaining control over you and your finances. The formula is 10-10-80, which stands for: save 10% / share 10% / spend 80%.

The best antidote for fear of financial ruin is to save money. There are several benefits to saving beyond the obvious financial benefits. Having money available for emergencies will make any emergency less of a full-blown crisis. Any emergency that looms less large in your mind will also generate less fear.

The discipline instilled by a regular saving program is also discipline that can be called on to get you through a crisis. People who save money on a regular basis suffer far less stress regarding their finances, compared to non-savers. Also, because their fears are under control, savers are far less likely to make an error in judgment during a moment of financial difficulty. As a bonus, they are able to take advantages of financial opportunities that are only available to those with ready cash.

The best antidote for greed is to share money. Greed is a vice that develops when someone craves as much as possible, without regard to how that may affect others. Sharing is the best method for keeping others in consideration. When you share, whether by giving to a church, a charity, or even to a friend or relative in need, you fight off the impulse to keep it all for yourself, which is the genesis of greed.

Greed is a habit that closely follows the law of diminishing returns. Greed as an ongoing pattern brings no real satisfaction to the greedy person; the marginal utility one gets from an extra dollar acquired through greed is almost non-existent. In contrast, there is almost no law of diminishing returns when it comes to sharing. Giving to others, especially those in need, feels as good the thousandth time you do it as it does the first. Giving is the gift that keeps on giving.

Why is the ratio 10-10-80? If people would save 10% of their income from their first paycheck onward, they should never have to worry about having enough for retirement. Furthermore, they will be able to handle almost any financial situation that arises between their first paycheck and their last one.

Sharing 10% is enough to make you appreciate the sacrifice you're making. The remaining 80% supports the individual. From a practical standpoint, it always makes sense not to spend all of your income maintaining your lifestyle. Living below your means via a 10-10-80 allocation is an effective way to limit spending.

Finally, there is no reason why you can't save and share more than 10% of your income, if circumstances allow it and you've a notion to do so.

BECOMING WHEALTHY

The landmark book *The Millionaire Next Door* offered some amazing insights into what millionaires are really like. According to *The Millionaire Next Door*, the single most important trait of the millionaire class is *frugality*. Frugality tends to have negative connotations. One of the synonyms for frugal is *parsimonious*, which, among its synonyms, are *stingy, ungenerous, miserly, mean, and tightfisted*.

Frugality simply means avoiding unnecessary expenditures. It does not mean avoiding necessary expenditures or any expenditure where the benefit outweighs the cost. To be frugal means to take your money seriously. Frugal is the opposite of wasteful, and no one gets to be a millionaire by being wasteful.

There is no way to build wealth without living below your means. Frugality is how you live below your means while still getting the most of every dollar you spend.

Those millionaires next door are quite willing to live below their means if it creates financial independence. They find nothing wrong with "stealth wealth," and most of them actually prefer that people think them to be less wealthy than they are.

Because of the way millionaires have been depicted by the media over decades, we have this misguided notion that millionaires care deeply about what the average person thinks of them and that they want very much to be admired for their wealth. Nothing could be further from the truth. Most millionaires would think *less* of you if they thought you were impressed mainly by their wealth. They would respond to your appreciation of the sacrifices they made to acquire their wealth, but not in your appreciation of the wealth itself.

One of the chapters in *The Millionaire Next Door* is titled "Economic Outpatient Care." The chapter focuses on two issues - the level of assistance that was provided to the millionaires and the level of assistance that they are providing to their adult children.

In the first case, very few millionaires received financial assistance. Fewer than 25% of them ever received more than $10,000 in total assistance; fewer than 20% inherited more than 10% of their wealth, and fewer than 10% ever received any ownership in a family business. These millionaires credit the fact that they *didn't* receive economic assistance as a key factor in their success.

Most of these millionaires feel that they would be doing their children a disservice to provide economic subsidies once they reach adulthood and are capable of supporting themselves. These subsidies lead to increased spending while decreasing initiative. In short, the more assistance that was given to capable adult children, the more they spent, the less they earned, and the less they saved.

In his book, *Toxic Charity - How Churches and Charities Hurt Those They Help (and How to Reverse it),* Robert Lupton chronicles the effects of one-way giving on communities around the world. He has spent decades doing charity work and has seen first-hand, both in the U.S. and abroad, the devastating effects that well-intentioned charity can have on the independence and dignity of the recipients of that charity. Lupton has developed an Oath for Compassionate Service, which includes:

- Never do for the poor what they have (or could have) the capacity to do for themselves.
- Limit one-way giving to emergency situations.

- Strive to empower the poor through employment, lending, and investing, using grants sparingly to reinforce achievements.
- Above all, do no harm.

Becoming fiscally stronger requires the exercise of our fiscal muscles, and doing for others what can and should be done by themselves causes the fiscal muscles of the recipients to atrophy from disuse.

If you are receiving some form of financial assistance, whether from parents, government, or others, it may be sapping your initiative in ways you may not recognize. Unless you are disabled to a great degree, it is likely that any such financial assistance is making you fiscally weaker, not stronger.

The issue here is not whether anyone is entitled to such assistance. The issue is what is best for your financial situation in the long run. When a parent pays for a child's college tuition, that is both right and expected. When that parent has that student move back home after graduation because there are no available jobs, that may be necessary, though that young adult should carry his/her own weight in maintaining the household. When a 35-year-old adult child is gainfully employed and is still receiving subsidies from his/her parents, assistance has gone from helpful to harmful. As difficult as it may be, all the parties have to face that reality and break the cycle of dependence and expectation that hurts everyone.

An income statement, along with a balance sheet, is one of the two most important financial statements for a household. The balance sheet gives you a snapshot of your assets, liabilities, and net worth at a moment in time. The income statement shows the income and expenses over a period of time, such as a month, a quarter, or a year. Creating an income statement provides an opportunity to determine where your income is being spent and also how income and expenses match up.

The income statement is revealing in many ways. For starters, it shows someone's priorities more clearly than any other piece of information; certainly more than anything they might say. If someone spends more on dining out than they contribute to their retirement accounts, that's not a good sign.

Expenses should equal income on an income statement because money is either saved or spent, and contributions to savings are listed under expense. The unaccounted-for expenses are typically items that are impulse purchases that may not leave a paper trail. Many people seem genuinely perplexed by this gap when they complete their income statement.

The main source of asset creation for most people is unspent income. Unspent income doesn't come about by accident - it comes about by designating money *not* to be spent before you designate any money *to* be spent.

People who have an income statement that has gaps, or worse, that has expenses exceeding income, almost always have one thing in common - they have never prepared a budget. To most people, preparing and using a budget is about as appealing as preparing and sticking to a diet. A budget is to your wealth as a diet is to your health. Both are paths that can lead you where you want to go.

One of the reasons so many people chafe at the idea of a budget is they feel that a budget will constrain them. No budget can constrain people. A budget is nothing more than words and numbers on a piece of paper or a spreadsheet; it won't be able to reel you in when you're at the mall and you see a pair of shoes "to die for."

The purpose of a budget is not to *restrict*, but to *illuminate*. One common appeal to get people to prepare a budget is that a budget lets you tell your dollars where to go, instead of leaving you wondering where they went. When people see clearly the patterns of their spending and how that spending can hurt them in the long run, they will instinctively begin to change that behavior on their own, without feeling pushed into doing it by a budget.

As we've learned, it's easier to be pulled to do something than to be pushed to it. A budget as restriction is like being pushed in a direction against your will. As soon as the opportunity presents itself, someone in the household will crack, and the budget will be busted. A budget as enlightenment will pull everyone in the household in a better financial direction. They will all be motivated for the right reasons, and their success is far more likely because changing spending patterns is something they *want* to do, not something they feel they *need* to do.

Once a budget is established, the budget can actually be liberating, rather than restricting. In creating a budget, a family prioritizes their spending. While many people applaud the idea of saving 10%, sharing 10%, and spending 80%, no one has ever accomplished that feat without a budget. Without a budget, money that is to be saved or shared will amount to whatever money is left at the end of the month. Of course, without a budget, there is no money left at the end of the month. A budget is the best way to put your future self at the head of the line to get a share of present earnings.

A budget is also liberating in that it can eliminate disputes, both internally and among family members, about how much should be spent in what categories and which categories take top priority. A budget sets priorities and limits, and it promotes self-control in spending and a shared vision for the family as a whole.

One of the most fundamental financial reports for any enterprise is the *balance sheet*. A balance sheet is a snapshot of an organization's financial position at a particular moment in time. The balance sheet has two sides, like the scales of justice. On one side are all the assets; on the other side are the liabilities. The goal is to have the assets outweigh the liabilities. Your personal balance sheet lets you determine your net worth by subtracting your liabilities from your assets.

The asset side of your balance sheet is like a sponge, something soft and squishy. The value of assets can change quickly and severely. Your assets can change size and get wrung out in much the same way as a sponge.

The liability side of your balance sheet is like granite, extremely hard and of definite size and shape. Almost all of the liabilities on your personal balance sheet were created by contracts drawn up by parties who were lending you money. The only way to reduce the liability is to pay down the debt.

One of the reasons so many Americans have found themselves in financial crisis in recent years is because no one ever pointed out the difference in assets and liabilities. No one ever told people who were taking on debt supported by the value of their assets that they were expecting sponges to counterbalance granite.

When we incur a liability, we should assume that the only way to reduce the liability is to use our income to pay it down. You can think of your liabilities as granite and your income as a hammer. The task is to pulverize the granite with the hammer. The smaller the hammer and the bigger the granite, the more trouble you'll have.

Even though, for many people, their home is their biggest single investment, viewing our home as an investment can get us into trouble. Thinking of our home through the lens of an investment can distort its real purpose and can cause us to do things with it that jeopardize the true purpose of our home.

The main purpose of our home is to serve as a *home*. When we can't depend on anything else, we need to be able to depend on our home, and this need is especially true for children. Realtors are quick to point to studies showing that owning a home has a great stabilizing effect on children.

After a home is purchased, the only other time its value should be relevant is on the day it is put up for sale. Ideally, those two days are years or decades apart. If the purchase price and other costs of a home are within the family budget, fluctuations in the value of the home are irrelevant to the family's ability to remain in the home. The family can keep making the payments and continue living in the home, and what others say the property is worth makes no difference.

In *The Blind Side*, Sandra Bulloch's family takes in a young man who becomes a highly recruited offensive lineman. She describes the reason that offensive lineman are important, and therefore well-paid, with an analogy. Every housewife knows that, after you pay the mortgage, the next bills to be paid are the insurance premiums. You don't risk losing your home by not paying the mortgage. You don't risk losing everything else by not paying for the insurance to protect it. The quarterback is like the home; the offensive linemen are his insurance.

There are many risks that we can and should insure against. These risks include, but are not limited to, losses caused by:
- Financial loss resulting from death (life insurance)
- Loss of income from illness or disability (disability insurance)
- Harm unintentionally inflicted on others (liability insurance)
- Damage to your vehicle (collision/comprehensive insurance)
- Injury/damage caused to you by another person's vehicle (uninsured/underinsured insurance)
- Major medical bills (health insurance)
- An extended illness or injury (long-term care insurance)
- Loss to real or personal property (homeowners insurance)

The more you have to lose, the more you need insurance. If you need a lot of insurance, you should feel good that you have a lot going for you that needs to be protected.

Many people equate insurance with gambling. They erroneously think that insurance is tantamount to making a bet on a potential loss. They may also take that line of thought out to the absurd conclusion that, if they don't have a loss, they've lost a bet with the insurance company. If you've ever had any kind of loss that was covered by insurance, you were no doubt very glad you had the insurance to help ease the pain of loss. However, if it were in your power, you would almost certainly have chosen for the loss to have never occurred.

Insurance is actually the opposite of gambling. When you gamble, you create a risk of loss where none existed before. When you buy insurance, you take the risk of a large and unpredictable loss and transfer it to the insurance company. In order to make this transfer, you accept the sure loss of paying them the insurance premium.

There are a couple of guidelines to follow when it comes to deciding whether you need insurance and how much insurance to get. First, don't risk a lot to save a little. For example, it would be foolish to risk a $400,000 house and all its contents to avoid spending a couple thousand dollars a year to insure it all. Second, don't spend a lot to reduce risk a little. As an example, extended warranties are far too expensive, relative to the protection they offer.

Insurance should be for those events that create a financial loss that creates a hardship. Paying a life insurance premium on the life of the breadwinner, so that the children won't be impoverished if he/she should die, is a smart use of insurance premium dollars. Paying extra on an auto policy to reduce the collision deductible from $500 to $100, when you can afford to pay the first $500 out-of-pocket, is a less-than-smart use of insurance premium dollars.

One of the greatest inducers of stress is uncertainty. More specifically, it isn't the uncertainty of events, but their consequences that creates stress. When you have a defense against the consequences of a bad scenario, the stress caused by uncertainty goes away.

Insurance doesn't protect you from an adverse event; it protects you from the financial consequences of an adverse event. We protect ourselves from many adverse events by our behavior. However, even careful people have bad things befall them. When bad things happen, insurance is there to help make what might be unbearable bearable.

Insurance is the foundation upon which financial strength is built. It won't matter how large you make the asset side of your balance sheet if those assets can all be lost due to events beyond your control.

The most basic car on the market today is better in every aspect than even the best cars of a couple of decades ago. A generation ago, it took care and regular maintenance to get a car to last much past 100,000 miles. Today, you don't even have to change spark plugs until the 100,000-mile mark. Because basic transportation today is hardly basic, one of the best ways to become fiscally stronger is to buy the car you need and to avoid the car you merely want.

To give you an idea the impact of buying too much car can have on your long-term fiscal health, let's compare two situations. She buys a practical car. He buys a slightly less practical car. His total car expenses are $100 per month more than hers. She puts that $100 difference into an S&P 500 mutual fund every month. They both follow this pattern for forty years. At the end, she has over a half-million dollars that he doesn't have.

We invest to create wealth, but do we really know how wealth is created? Surprisingly, wealth is created with only two ingredients - work and delayed gratification. Only work creates something of value where nothing of value previously existed. Only delayed gratification prevents something of value from being consumed in the present and gives it the opportunity to grow into something even more substantial in the future. Creating wealth isn't complicated. Work is something most of us do for decades; it's the delayed gratification part that trips most people up on the way to wealth. The magic formula for creating wealth is simple - work, earn, invest, repeat. It's not complicated, though it's not easy either, unless you develop the habit.

When it comes to determining if something is an investment, remember this requirement - an investment must perform work. Many "investments" are little more than bets; they are a zero-sum game. Because an investment performs work, it provides the first ingredient in the creation of wealth. An investment does not gain value by taking it from someplace else. It creates its own value through the work it performs.

Here are some examples to illustrate:
- Stock in a gold mining company is an investment; gold is not. A gold mining company creates wealth by extracting and processing a precious metal. Gold itself just sits there, its value based on supply and demand beyond its control.
- A rental house is an investment; idle land is not. The house does work by providing shelter to tenants. The land, like gold, just sits there, its owner hoping that someone will want to pay more for it than he/she did.
- Stock in a casino is an investment; lottery tickets are not. A casino provides entertainment to its patrons, and some of that entertainment is in the form of gambling. Lottery tickets are a zero-sum game where all the winnings have to come from the losses of others.

Would you rather be an owner or a loaner? You may not have been posed such a question before, but it goes to determining if you are more likely to prefer owning stocks or bonds, which are the most commonly held classes of investment assets after one's personal home.

When you own stock in a corporation, you become a part-owner of the corporation. Your liability is limited to the amount of your investment in the stock of that company, although all of that investment is theoretically at risk. If the company goes bankrupt and the value of the stock goes to zero, you lose all of your investment.

You also stand last in line after creditors, employees, and others to receive any of the income from the corporation. If there's no money left after everyone else has been paid, too bad. On the other hand, whatever is left after everyone has been paid is yours.

Sometimes the corporation will give out part of those profits to you in the form of dividends. Most of the profits of a corporation are kept by the company (retained earnings) and are used to grow the company and increase the value of your stock. When you are the owner of a company, whether it is a small business you started or a Fortune 500 company in which you are a stockholder, you bear most of the risk if things go badly. You also have the potential for unlimited rewards if things go really well.

When you are a bond holder, you are loaning money to the issuer of the bond, whether it is a corporation or a government. When bonds are issued, an interest rate is stated that the bondholder will pay. There is also a redemption date for the bond, at which time the original amount of the bond is repaid to the bondholder. Interest payments are made on a regular basis over the term of the bond.

Bondholders stand near the front of the line when it comes to getting paid. Bondholders must receive all the interest and principal payments that are due them before any money can be paid to stockholders. Bondholders also stand near the front of the line when it comes to claiming the assets of the corporation. If it gets to that point, the bonds and the business itself may not be worth much, though.

Even though bondholders face less risk than stockholders, there are risks nonetheless. If the issuer of the bond goes bankrupt, all of your investment could be lost. There is also the risk that the issuer will be unable to make timely interest payments, due to financial difficulties. Then there's what is known as interest-rate risk. Recall that inflation pushes interest rates higher, as investors need to stay ahead of inflation if they are going to be persuaded to invest. If inflation rises during the time a bond is in force, its value may drop.

Because bonds, as a group, have less risk than stocks as a group, they have also had a lower return over long periods of time. Both have the potential to become worthless, though bondholders do stand in front of stockholders when it comes to getting paid. Bondholders also have a ceiling. They will not receive more from the bond issuer than the stated rate of interest. Stockholders have less of a floor of protection than bondholders. They also have no ceiling in terms of how much of a return they might receive.

Diversifying your investments lowers your risk without lowering your returns. There are plenty of good investment opportunities in every asset class, so it makes sense to not pile all your money into any single one. It also makes sense to not put all your money into any one asset class. Whole asset classes can hit the skids for a prolonged period of time, real estate being one example. When you diversify, there is likely to be some investment you own that is not performing particularly well at that moment. However, diversification is the best method to avoid the kind of wealth destruction from which you might never recover.

When you look at your investment portfolio, how much of it could you afford to lose permanently? If, like most people, you said that a permanent loss of more than 5% of your investment portfolio would be unacceptable, then you should have no more than 5% of your investment portfolio in any one investment. The guideline is simple - never invest any more in any one thing than you can afford to *permanently lose*.

When Social Security was enacted in 1935, the average worker began working at age 15 and worked for 50 years to age 65. That's not entirely true, because half the workers died before reaching 65; those who made it lived an average of 5 more years.

Today, workers begin working in their early-to-mid-20's, and they are eligible for Social Security at 62. At age 62, there is better than a 50-50 chance that at least one partner in a marriage will still be around at age 90. In 1935, the average ratio of years worked to years retired was 10 to 1. Today that ratio is less than 2 to 1, which is why the entire Social Security system is in danger.

Over the last 30 years there has also been a massive change in private pension programs. In the past, almost every retirement plan was a *defined benefit plan*. In a defined benefit plan, the provider of the plan (typically the employer) agrees to provide a defined benefit to their retirees, regardless of the cost. In these plans, the risk is assumed by the plan provider. Those risks include uncertainty regarding life expectancies, cost of living increases, and other variables that can make a plan far more expensive than was anticipated.

Since the 1980's, the defined benefit plan has almost completely disappeared from the private sector and has been replaced by *defined contribution plans*. In a defined contribution plan, the provider agrees to provide a defined contribution to an employee's retirement account. In these plans, the risk of uncertainty is shifted from the provider to the employee. The employee typically must determine how much should be funded to the retirement account, as well as making all the investment decisions regarding that account.

Longer periods of retirement, combined with a shift in responsibility of funding that retirement to the individual, is perhaps the greatest financial challenge facing Americans today. In most cases, workers will need to start saving at least 10% of their earnings from the start of their careers if they hope to retire at an age and standard of living that comes close to their expectations.

Many employers prime the pump for their workers by offering some kind of match to an employee's retirement contributions. The employee still has to fund the lion's share of his/her retirement, but the employer's contribution helps.

Funding your retirement account over a period of decades enables you to take advantage of one of the greatest financial inventions since compound interest - dollar-cost averaging. When you invest the same amount every month in the same investment, there will be times that you buy when the price is high and times that you buy when the price is low. Since the amount you invest every month stays the same, the number of shares you buy every month will vary, depending on the price. When the price is low, you will buy more shares; when the price is high, you will buy fewer shares.

Because of the long time frame involved in saving for retirement, short-term market fluctuations will not affect the outcome. When you are able to stop worrying about short-term volatility and even embrace it, you can invest in the asset classes that have demonstrated the best returns over long periods of time. Stocks have historically led that field.

Stocks have historically outpaced bonds by 2-3% per year over long periods. If a 25-year-old worker starts by contributing $5,000 to a retirement account in the first year, increases that amount 4% per year, works until age 65, and gets an average 8% return over that period, there will be $2.125 million in the account on retirement day. If that same employee chooses a more conservative portfolio that provides a consistent 6% return, the amount in the account on retirement day will be $1.371 million. This 2% difference in average annual return creates a 35% difference in retirement funds when it's time to retire.

Many people want to know just how much they need to have in their retirement account in order to retire comfortably. That number is based on many factors, including:
- Age at retirement and life expectancy
- Other sources of income
- Outstanding debt and other obligations
- Investment return during retirement

Here is a very general number that can give you an idea of what it takes to begin retirement in comfort and to remain there - *20 to 25*. On the day you retire, if you have 20 to 25 times the amount you will need to withdraw from your retirement account during the first year in that account, you are likely to be fine. To put this in perspective, in order to draw $50,000 from your retirement account in the first year, you should have $1 million to $1.25 million in the account.

You should withdraw no more than 4-5% of the account each year for the first 10 years, assuming about a 25-year retirement. You should also not get too conservative with your investments during retirement. Inflation will continue throughout retirement.

When we look at the immediate situation we and our families face, it can be difficult to make the necessary sacrifices to invest for our retirement. Many parents will not fund a 401(k) at work because they are building a college fund for a child instead. Many parents even take money out of retirement accounts (incurring heavy penalties) in order to fund things like a home purchase or education for children. Well-intentioned as these moves may be, they are likely to create serious financial problems in the long run.

You, and only you, are responsible for your financial security when you are no longer able to work. You may think that you can simply work longer. That assumes you will be physically able to work longer and you will have skills at that age that have market value.

You may think that your children can repay you for funding their education by letting you live with them when you're old. That situation is fine if everyone agrees to it voluntarily. Neither party wants to feel that they are forced by circumstances into such an arrangement. If you have to decline a request for financial assistance because you have to fund your retirement first, point out that you are doing so to make sure that you will not be a burden to anyone in the future. Preparing for your future is not selfish. It can actually be an act of kindness and discipline when the immediate situation cries for attention.

Becoming fiscally stronger is the result of doing many things a little better than they've been done in the past. Becoming a little smarter, a little more disciplined, and a little more proactive can make a huge difference in your fiscal strength.

Becoming WHEALTHY

Health is the greatest gift,
Contentment the greatest wealth,
Faithfulness the best relationship.
              -Gautama Buddha

Once upon a time, there was an entertainer named Michael Jackson, who was both handsome and rich. He has been recognized as the most successful entertainer of all time by Guinness World Records. His lifetime earnings are estimated at $750 million dollars; though, at his death in 2009, his estimated debt totaled $400 million. Before repeated plastic surgeries drastically altered his appearance, Michael Jackson was considered the sexiest man alive by millions of adoring fans. In his twenties, Michael Jackson had health and wealth that few people could imagine. Yet, when he died a premature death at age 50, he had neither.

When we see someone who is good-looking and who makes a lot of money, one of two emotions usually springs up - admiration or envy. At his peak, people admired Jackson; as he began to squander his health and wealth, the admiration turned to disdain.

We hate to see people squander things that we may have no hope of ever attaining. However, we can easily misinterpret what we see. When we see someone who has a large income or who simply spends prodigiously, we assume that person is wealthy. When we see someone who possesses physical beauty, we assume that person also enjoys phenomenal health. Beauty is to health as income is to wealth; the former may be an indicator of the latter, but it is in no way a guarantor.

BECOMING WHEALTHY

Aesop, of "Aesop's Fables" fame, said nearly 2,500 years ago, "Beware, lest you lose the substance by grabbing at the shadow." When we seek beauty and income and ignore health and wealth, we can lose the substance by grabbing at the shadow. Becoming whealthy first requires that you know what you are going after and why you are going after it.

More than anything else, becoming whealthy enables you to live life on your terms. When your health is an asset instead of a liability, you can partake in more of the pleasurable activities of life. You are also less likely to have to rely on others for care and assistance, which compromises their ability to live life on their terms. When your wealth is sufficient to adequately support you, you can, within reason, do the things you want to do. You also don't have to rely on others, whether individually or through government programs, to support you.

Everything in life has a point of diminishing returns. For that reason, the optimum amount of something is rarely the maximum amount. Surprisingly, this truth is even true of something like wealth. The addictive quality of many things, even things that are good for us, can cause us to keep acquiring them long past the point where they serve a useful purpose. Also, the effort to continue acquiring can have a detrimental effect on other aspects of life. In the process of becoming whealthy, it's important to establish what you consider to be optimal levels of health and wealth. Once those levels are reached, it's then time to look for other areas where you can improve your quality of life.

Remember Maslow's Hierarchy of Needs - once the lower level needs are taken care of, it's time to move on to the higher levels. The people I know who have enjoyed the best health over the longest periods of time did not obsess over their health. These people understand the first rule of good health - if you abuse it, you lose it. Beyond that, they are satisficers, not maximizers. They take all *reasonable* steps to maintain their health. Then they go about their lives, which tend to be both fulfilling and of long duration.

Many, but not all, of the people I just described have also applied the same philosophy to their wealth. First, they don't abuse their wealth by making foolish or risky investments. They also don't abuse their wealth by squandering it on things that imply status or provide fleeting pleasure. They understand the hierarchy of needs. Once they have sufficient wealth to take care of the lower levels, they devote energy to self-actualization, which does not have to be capital intensive. These people have attained a balance in their lives that we can all emulate. They have attained and maintained health and wealth. They have also learned that their whealth is not just the end, but also the means to an end. By becoming whealthy, they have enabled themselves to become more, to become anything they set their mind to becoming.

Becoming whealthy is a desirable end in itself, for many reasons. At its most basic, being healthy is better than being sick, and being wealthy is better than being poor. Being healthy and wealthy doesn't make you a better person, but it is a more desirable state.

Becoming whealthy also opens up opportunities that only become obvious once that state is reached. Maslow's Hierarchy of Needs is typically represented as a pyramid:

BECOMING WHEALTHY

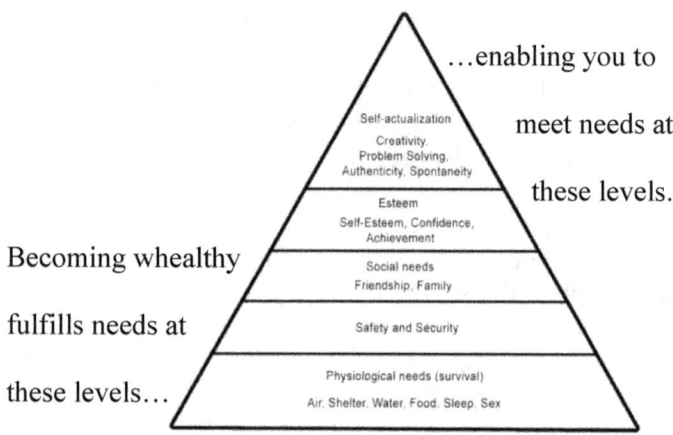

Becoming whealthy fulfills needs at these levels... ...enabling you to meet needs at these levels.

Becoming whealthy enables you to build a solid foundation at the lower two levels of the pyramid. You are then able to address the higher level of needs with confidence, knowing that the lower levels that support them won't let you down. Whealth is not a higher level need, but meeting higher level needs is difficult, if not impossible, without whealth.

Here are fifty specific things you can do that will not only help you become whealthy, but that can also help you enjoy greater success and happiness in almost any aspect of your life:

1. **Take a personality evaluation**. Before you can know what to do, you need to know who you are. The Myers-Briggs Type Indicator (MBTI) is one of the best methods of measuring key aspects of your personality. The MBTI helps you understand how you relate to others, how you learn, evaluate, prioritize, and make decisions. It also helps you understand how you are motivated. A personality evaluation can provide essential guidance on the best

methods to employ in your efforts to become whealthy.
2. **Diagnose your character strengths**. The Authentic Happiness Testing Center offers an evaluation that identifies 25 specific character strengths and ranks them in order from your greatest assets to your greatest potential liabilities. Knowing your greatest strengths and weaknesses enables you to focus your efforts on maximizing the gain from your greatest strengths and minimizing the damage from your greatest weaknesses. Both the personality and character strength evaluations help you know yourself better, which can help you concentrate your efforts where they will do the most good to become whealthy.
3. **Learn to recognize the stages of progress**. Progress never occurs in a straight line. At the beginning, you are full of energy and enthusiasm. As you get close to reaching your goal, you feel pride in your pending achievement, which keeps you moving forward toward that goal. In the middle, though, there can be weeks, months, and even years that can feel like nothing but an endless grind. The worthiness of most endeavors and the sustained effort it takes to achieve them are usually in direct proportion to each other. Recognizing that there will be long periods of just plain old work is an important factor in getting through those periods.
4. **Find your inspiration**. Inspiration can come from anywhere. Sometimes it comes from the example of others; sometimes it comes from events; sometimes it just comes from inside your own heart and soul. Regardless of the source, inspiration pulls you in a positive direction. Because inspiration is pulling

you, you are not really doing any work at this stage. The more timeless the inspiration, the longer and farther it can pull you, which enables your own efforts to achieve more. Inspirations that come from timeless sources like faith, family, and patriotism are the types that will still be helping you when the work is the hardest.

5. **Motivate yourself**. While inspiration pulls you forward, motivation pushes you. For example, you may have become inspired to be a writer by reading great literature, but you will have to motivate yourself to take steps to become that writer. One of those steps may be to earn a degree in writing, which will require you to attend classes, write papers, and take exams. Inspiration can help you maintain focus on the big prize, but motivation is what enables you to initiate the tactics that will earn that prize. Motivation can be as simple as rewarding yourself with a new pair of shoes if you get an 'A' on the essay you're writing. Motivation is often the little rewards that keep you moving when the big prize seems far off in the future.

6. **Find work that inspires**. Work is probably a big part of your life. The best way to be continually inspired is to be continually inspired by the things that are already a big part of your life, such as work. Too many people merely have jobs; too few have a calling. While you may never be fortunate enough to work in a field that you view as a true calling, all work offers the opportunity for service to others. True inspiration takes you beyond what you can do for yourself to what you can do for others. By looking at your work, any work, as an opportunity to benefit mankind, you can become inspired by it.

7. **Find a workplace that motivates.** A motivating workplace is one that provides challenging work, recognition, responsibility, and opportunity for achievement. Such a workplace attends to the higher levels of your hierarchy of needs, while giving adequate attention to the lower levels, too. If you're like most people, you want the opportunity at work to experience mastery of a task, to have autonomy to do your job the best way you see fit, and to interact with others in a supportive environment. In such an environment, success is almost inevitable.
8. **Don't use money as inspiration or motivation.** Money never inspires because it is inanimate, and it doesn't motivate well because its effects can be like a drug - you get an initial rush, then you crash and need an even bigger dose of money to get motivated next time. Compensation should be adequate enough so that compensation isn't an issue. Money is our main method of compensation, and to compensate means to offset or to counterbalance. Inspiration and motivation don't offset; they raise up, which is more than money can do.
9. **Think absolutely, not relatively.** Most millionaires are millionaires because they live below their means. Most millionaires don't care at all what other people assume about their wealth or lifestyle. They don't compare themselves to others, and they don't pay attention to those who do. If you spend your time making comparisons to others, you are not going to improve your performance. You will only frustrate yourself when you compare yourself to "superiors," while giving yourself a false sense of superiority when you compare yourself to "inferiors." When

you set goals, don't aim to be *the* best; aim to do *your* best.
10. **Before asking who, what, when, where, or how questions, answer the question, "Why?"** To know why you are doing something is to understand its purpose. You can never be properly inspired and motivated to do anything unless you know the reasons why that thing is worth doing in the first place. Questions that deal with who, what, when, where, and how deal with tactics, and tactics take a secondary position to purpose. Also, when the question of why you are doing something is adequately answered, the tactical questions of who, what, when, where and how become easier to answer.
11. **Focus on relationships first**. The people who consistently express a high level of happiness in their lives are people who have a strong network of positive relationships with other people. Supporting the notion that relationships form a key ingredient to human happiness, the largest area of regret for the dying is the relationships they neglected to maintain or cultivate. Without meaningful relationships, without people in your life whom you care about deeply, you are far less likely to be inspired to accomplish much in life. Even if you become a success, it won't feel like success if you can't share it with others.
12. **Give first, but expect reciprocity**. The best relationships are based on five attributes: respect, shared experience, mutual enjoyment, trust, and reciprocity. Relationships always begin by one person giving to another. If you want a relationship, you have to be willing to give first and continue

giving. However, if a relationship is to last, there has to be a balance in the giving; there has to be reciprocity. Giving without receiving turns you into a victim; taking without giving turns you into a parasite. Our innate desire for reciprocity helps keep relationships from becoming one-sided.

13. **Create win-win opportunities**. The desire for reciprocity makes relationships about cooperation, rather than competition. The best relationships are those in which everyone feels they are better off for being in the relationship. When everyone feels like they have gained something, you have a win-win situation. It isn't necessary for everyone to gain equally every time. The main thing is that everyone feels they have won something and that no one else has gained something at another's expense. The creation of whealth is based on win-win. We can all become healthier simultaneously. In fact, it's easier that way. The creation of wealth is win-win. Where wealth is concerned, win-lose is not the creation of wealth, but merely the transfer of wealth.

14. **Beware of loneliness**. A few deep friendships are far more valuable than dozens of acquaintances. Social media has given us the ability to claim hundreds of "friends," but very few of them would act as a friend when you most needed one. True friendships are developed over time and through personal contact. Our desire to be individualistic can also impede our ability to form bonds with others, especially as part of a group. Individualism is often a precursor to loneliness. Loneliness leads to a variety of health problems. People who live isolated lives also lead shorter lives.

15. **Develop the habits of self-control.** Self-control is a better predictor of and a more necessary ingredient to success than intelligence. Self-control, or the lack of it, has a greater effect on your health and wealth than any other single factor. The ability to delay gratification is one of the most important examples of self-control; it is also one of the two ingredients used to create wealth (work is the other). Self-control is a habit that is developed over time. The earlier you begin to develop a habit of self-control, the greater your self-control will be and the easier it will be to utilize it.
16. **Develop the muscles of willpower.** Willpower is summoned when there is an out-of-the-ordinary circumstance that requires you to act in a manner counter to your first impulse. Willpower can be used to resist the temptation to eat a quart of ice cream or to make yourself run an extra two miles. Willpower is like a muscle. It gets both stronger and more exhausted with use. You have a single source of willpower, and its volume is finite. When you use willpower for one purpose, there will be less willpower in the short term if you need to tap it again.
17. **Recognize when you're most vulnerable.** Your willpower can be drained by everything from low blood sugar to making a lot of decisions in a short period of time. Stress in one area of your life that depletes willpower, such as work, can leave you with little willpower to deal with family matters when you get home. Any time you are tired, hungry, or in pain, your willpower is depleted. You become more likely to give into temptation or do something you will regret later. If you know your willpower is

drained, it's best to avoid situations that will require willpower until you build your levels back up. Usually food and rest will resupply the willpower tank.

18. **Earn self-esteem**. Self-esteem is not given. It is earned by the individual through accomplishment. Self-esteem movements of recent years have led young people to believe that they are worthy of adulation by their mere existence. When they become adults, they find a very different world where only achievement is valued. Developing a list of accomplishments, which can only happen through the exercise of self-control and willpower, will lead to *real* self-esteem - the kind that doesn't crumble the first time someone criticizes or mocks you.

19. **Develop a personal mission statement**. Your mission statement encompasses your personal philosophy and puts into words why you think you were put on this planet. Your mission statement serves as your guiding star as you navigate the currents of life. Whenever you have a conflict or a crisis in your life, you can look back to your personal mission statement to guide you as to the proper path to take. Your personal mission statement is a necessary prerequisite to setting goals, and it will make the process of setting goals far easier.

20. **Set goals**. Your success in becoming whealthy will not occur by accident. You will have to develop a plan to get there. Setting goals is how you chart the course to achieve what you desire. Goals should be challenging, but attainable. Goals must also be quantifiable. For a goal to have meaning, you should be able to have a clear way of knowing if you have achieved that goal. To that end, each goal should be

measurable with time and an amount, such as setting a goal to lose 20 pounds in 6 months, as opposed to merely setting a goal to "lose weight."

21. **Focus on inputs, not outcomes**. The goals you set for yourself should be behavioral goals, first and foremost. You have a limited ability to control outcomes or effects. You have an almost unlimited ability to control inputs or causes. Part of the frustration people have with unmet goals is they focus solely on outcomes and ignore inputs. If your goal is to lose 20 pounds in 6 months, the weight loss is an outcome; you also need a behavioral goal that addresses the inputs necessary to achieve the weight loss. Such goals might be to walk 2 miles a day and to abstain from ice cream.

22. **Be a piranha, not a python**. Big audacious goals may be inspiring, but you may find yourself overwhelmed by their size when you get up close. Rather than trying to swallow a huge goal in one gulp, like a python, you can maintain motivation and momentum by taking many small bites, like a piranha. A big audacious goal like running a marathon is inspiring, but no one does that all at once. Achieving smaller goals on the way, like completing a 5k, a 10k, and a 20k race, will lead to achieving the big audacious goal without choking on it.

23. **Understand how habits develop**. Humans have evolved to be as efficient as possible. To that end, our brains have developed the capacity to create habits. Habits are your brain's method of minimizing the thought needed to complete tasks. Your brain does not give preference to good or bad habits, though humans find it far easier and more rewarding

in the short term to create bad habits. Bad habits, such as overeating, typically begin unconsciously, or at least unintentionally. Good habits, such as exercising, typically require more effort to get out of the starting gate. However, once established, it takes no more effort to maintain a good habit than a bad one.

24. **Change the routine between the cue and the reward**. Habits are loops that include a cue, a routine, a reward, and a craving that powers the loop. For a habit like smoking, the cue may be the completion of a meal; the routine is smoking; the reward may be a feeling of relaxation. There is no need to change the cue or the reward, only the routine in between. Since it's the reward you seek, not the routine, a habit like smoking can be broken when a different routine, such as walking, brings a similar reward.

25. **Embrace peer pressure for a good cause**. Relying on others to keep you on the straight and narrow is something humans have done since the beginning of our existence. Those who believe in God have fewer behavioral problems, in part because they feel the need to please, or at least to not displease, the Almighty. Belonging to a group that advocates a healthy lifestyle will create a desire to conform by leading a healthy lifestyle, too. Embracing good influences is just as important to becoming whealthy as rejecting bad ones.

26. **Apply the 80/20 principle**. In becoming whealthy, it's helpful to understand that 80% of your success will come from just 20% of your inputs and that 80% of your problems will come from 20% of your inputs (or lack thereof). Understanding your

character strengths can enable you to harness the potential of your greatest strengths to minimize the damage caused by your greatest weaknesses. You should also ignore the other areas that will have a negligible effect on outcomes. Applying the 80/20 principle simply makes you more effective and efficient.
27. **Practice Kaizen**. Kaizen is the Japanese philosophy of continual improvement. Kaizen is proactive, rather than reactive. Kaizen takes a long-term view. Small improvements, accumulated and incorporated over years and decades, are how you get and remain ahead of the competition. Kaizen is about taking small steps to improve whenever the opportunity presents itself and to always be looking for ways to make improvements, even in areas that seem to be working fine in the present.
28. **Expend energy to create more energy**. Because your body was designed to handle more activity than you probably give it, it doesn't know its true capabilities. When you don't expend much energy, your body's ability to exert energy is depleted. The more active you are, the more active you are capable of being. This rule also applies in relationships. If you expend care and consideration of others, you increase your ability to give both, not just in yourself, but in others, too.
29. **Beware of the paradox of choice**. As much as we all want and even demand choices, there is a negative correlation between the number of choices offered and the quality of decisions made about those choices. The more choices you have, the more information you have to process and the more decisions you have to make. Too many choices can

lead you to take the default position or to abstain from participating at all. When it comes to important decisions, such as funding retirement, too many choices can lead to decisions that can have a serious negative impact on your life.
30. **Differentiate between needs and wants**. To make proper choices, you have to be able discern between what you truly need and what you merely want. Your needs are fairly limited, but your wants can be infinite. When you want something very badly, it can be tempting to reclassify it as a need to enable you to get it without feeling guilty. While there is nothing wrong with satisfying your wants, they should never take priority over your needs, which include your needs in the future. It is those future needs that are often sacrificed to satisfy current wants.
31. **Don't maximize; satisfy**. Everything reaches a point of diminishing returns, including the effort it takes to create certain outcomes. The people who are the happiest *and* the most successful are those who can recognize when it's time to focus energies on other endeavors that will be more rewarding. The maximum amount of something is also rarely the optimal amount of something. The best amount of wealth is not the most amount of wealth. The reward of acquiring the maximum amount of anything is rarely worth the effort needed to acquire it. Maximum rarely has an upper limit, either.
32. **Minimize negative emotions**. In looking at a comprehensive list of human emotions, there seem to be far more negative than positive ones. Negative emotions seem to come more naturally and more spontaneously, which may be part of our survival

instinct. Some negative emotions, like fear, are helpful at times and are even necessary for survival. However, most negative emotions create poor emotional health, which can lead to poor physical health. Negative emotions can be harder to control and, when left uncontrolled, can damage your health, your finances, and your relationships.

33. **Generate positive emotions**. Positive emotions, like gratitude and humor, can counteract the negative effects of negative emotions, and they have documented healing powers. Negative emotions can create a downward spiral. These emotions lead to negative outcomes, which reinforce negative emotions. Positive emotions create positive outcomes, which makes it much easier to maintain positive emotions like optimism and gratitude. Emotions can become a habit, and they tend to follow the established trend. Focusing on making positive emotions a habit increases your chances for positive outcomes.

34. **Use the sails and rudder together**. Your thinking part is the rudder, and your emotional parts are the sails. You need your emotions to get moving. However, without thought to act as the rudder, your emotions can cause you to sail off the edge of the earth. Though no one is willing to admit it, almost everyone makes decisions with their emotions and then justifies those decisions with whatever logic they can muster. To suppress all emotion is to pull in the sails, which means you'll go nowhere. To suppress thought is to leave the rudder unmanned. You will never sail to your destination without a skillful use of both sails and rudder.

35. **Keep success in perspective**. Success and failure are two sides of the same coin. They are also nouns, not adjectives. You may achieve success or experience failure; neither one means that you *are* a success or a failure. Achieving success often leaves a feeling of disappointment. You expect success to lead to happiness, but in reality happiness leads to success. The happiness that success brings lies not in the ultimate achievement, but in the effort made to reach that achievement. If you think about your past successes, the journey to reach that goal was probably more fulfilling than reaching the destination.
36. **Develop rational optimism**. With any worthwhile endeavor, you will likely experience enthusiasm at the beginning and satisfaction toward the end. In the middle you may want to quit many times. Rational optimism is simply the belief that you will ultimately accomplish your goals, as well as the recognition that it won't always be easy. Those who are pessimistic about their eventual success will give up at the first obstacle. Those who are naïve about the obstacles will believe them to be insurmountable. Rational optimism does not mean you avoid obstacles; it means you transcend them.
37. **Pay yourself first regarding time management**. We all get the same ration of time each day - 24 hours. Nothing else in life is distributed as equally. How you allocate each 24 hours is the largest single factor in becoming whealthy. If you don't allocate your time to improve your condition, no one else will devote time to your cause. Also, if you don't allocate the necessary time to maintain and improve your condition, you won't be in a position to help

others with your time, talent, or treasure when they need your help. Paying yourself with adequate amounts of time for sleep, exercise, socializing, and solitude are the best investments you can make toward becoming whealthy.

38. **Ignore the talking heads**. Whether it's TV commercials that try to sell you medications you don't need or TV pundits who scream about the latest crisis du jour, it's easy to believe you are far sicker and in far greater danger than you actually are. If you stop and think about all the dire predictions that have been made in recent years, then look at how few actually came to pass, then look at how even fewer actually affected you, you begin to realize that all that noise is designed to serve the interests of the noisemakers, not you. You can affect your condition in a far more positive way by reallocating the time spent with the talking heads to some of the areas mentioned in number 37.

39. **Laugh your ass off**. Laughter not only releases positive chemicals in the body that have remarkable healing powers, the act of laughter itself is good exercise. Clubs have even been created around the world that utilize self-triggering laughter to improve overall well-being and as a form of exercise. Even if your laughter is not induced by something funny, the body has the same positive reaction to that laughter. Whenever you are feeling particularly stressed, the best prescription may be to take three Stooges and get a good night's sleep.

40. **Generate horsepower and torque**. Aerobic exercise is your body's way of generating horsepower, which is a measure of moving weight over distance divided by time. You generate

horsepower when you swim or jog. Strength training is your body's way of generating torque, which is a measure of effort used to move or turn something. A proper exercise routine incorporates both aerobic and strength training. Just like an engine needs to be able to both move from a standstill and maintain a steady speed, your body needs to be able to sustain activity, as well as provide bursts of power as needed.

41. **Play games**. It's not a coincidence that the best athletes in the world play games for a living. When you do something because you have to, it's work; when you do it because you want to, it's play. Playing games is the best way to make sure that exercise feels like play instead of work. Playing games also adds a social component to exercise, which is a powerful inducement to keep it up. Friendly competition can also act as an incentive, as long as winning does not overshadow the health and social aspects of playing games.

42. **Go to bed**. Studies show that 95% of adults need 7 to 8 hours of sleep per night. Studies also show that most adults don't get that much sleep. Taking time away from sleep to work is a poor investment. Studies show that productivity drops far more than the additional work time covers, if that time comes at the expense of a proper amount of sleep. Inadequate sleep has adverse effects on your health. It also affects the quality of your work, which can affect your ability to increase your income. Sleep and dreams are also essential ingredients in the brain's ability to be creative.

43. **Ease yourself into a smaller body**. Your body doesn't like to be shocked, as you have probably

learned over the years. If you suddenly decide to go from couch potato to gym rat or if you decide to lose 30 pounds before the class reunion next month, you will shock your body, and it will retaliate. You have to ease into exercise and weight loss programs so your body doesn't think you're trying to kill it through starvation or physical strain. You can make all the physical changes you want to make, and if they are changes for the better, your body will cooperate. Your body just wants you to do it over time, not do it overnight.

44. **Understand what money represents**. While we represent money with currency, money itself represents purchasing power. You may be like most people and see money as currency, not as purchasing power. This mistake can lead you to sacrifice the purchasing power of your money in order to protect the currency that represents it. If inflation runs at 5% this year and your money earns 2% during that time, you will have more currency at the end of the year, but less purchasing power. Since money exists only to be spent, whether on investments, luxuries, or necessities, the only measure of importance is how much your money will buy, not how much currency you possess.

45. **Recognize your risk tolerance**. Risk and reward move in the same direction. In order to get a larger reward, you have to be willing to accept more risk. This correlation applies whether you are talking about investments or thinking about going into business for yourself. The lure of higher rewards might cause you to take on more risk than you are capable of handling. You might invest in risky ventures that go bust, costing you everything you

risked. When it comes to risk and reward, your risk tolerance determines the potential reward. The potential reward does not determine your risk tolerance.

46. **Save 10%; share 10%; spend 80%**. Fear and greed are the two most damaging emotions when it comes to creating and maintaining wealth. If you save 10% of your income, you will reduce fear because you have a cash reserve to protect you. You have also developed discipline that can help you control your fears. If you share 10% of your income, you will keep greed at bay because you are thinking about others, not just about acquiring more for yourself. Allocating your income in this manner actually strengthens your financial position in the long run.

47. **Practice frugality**. The only way you can create wealth is to make sure that your expenses are less than your income. Frugality is a virtue that helps assure that you spend no more than you need to and that you get the best value for the money you do spend. Frugality does not mean being tightfisted. It means that you make sure you spend money wisely. You act as a steward of your money, and you treat it with respect because you appreciate the sacrifices you made to earn it. When you see people spending money frivolously, you can be sure of one of two things: either they are spending money they don't have, or they will have no money to spend before long.

48. **Liberate yourself with a budget**. A budget does not restrict your spending. It liberates you from financial stress. A budget can serve to illuminate your spending and show you the difference between how you *are* spending your money and how you *want to*

be spending your money. Unless someone else is imposing a budget on you, you should not feel that a budget is restricting or punishing. A budget simply directs your money to go where you tell it to go. If you don't give your money specific directions, it will go to the first thing that attracts it, which is almost never the best place for it to go.

49. **Play defense first**. It's hard enough to accumulate wealth. It makes no sense not to protect your assets once you've acquired them or not to protect your ability to acquire more assets in the future. Life and disability insurance defend against the loss of income due to disability or death. Liability insurance defends against the loss of everything if you do something that harms another person. Health insurance defends against medical bills that could bankrupt you. Property insurance defends against the loss of all the stuff you've managed to accumulate to date and will accumulate in the future. If you don't defend your assets, you'll eventually lose them.

50. **Invest for the long run**. If you're like most people, most of your investing is done to accumulate money for retirement. That money will not get spent, on average, until you are about 75 years old. You are probably a long way from 75, which means the short-term ups and downs of the stock market are irrelevant to your long-term plans. Those who keep a long-term perspective on their investing fare better on average than those who do a lot of active trading or who try to time the ups and downs of the markets. Remember the fable of the tortoise and the hare - slow and steady wins the race.

REFERENCES

BOOKS/PAPERS

Ariely, Dan; *Predictably Irrational*; 2008; Harper Collins

Austin, Andrew D. & Hungerford, Thomas L.; *The Market Structure of Health Insurance*; 2009; CRS Report for Congress

Bartlett, Donald L. & Steele, James B.; *Critical Condition*; 2004; Doubleday

Baumeister, Roy F. & Tierney, John; *Willpower*; 2011; Penguin Press

Covey, Stephen R.; *The 7 Habits of Highly Effective People*; 1989; Fireside Books

Duhigg, Charles; *The Power of Habit*; 2012; Random House

Easterbrook, Gregg; *The Progress Paradox*; 2003; Random House

Edlund, Matthew, MD; *Healthy Without Health Insurance*; 2012; Circadian Press

Eisenberg, Lee; *The Number*; 2006; Free Press

Fishman, Ted C.; *Shock of Gray*; 2010; Scribner

Frederickson, Barbara L.; *The Value of Positive Emotions*; 2003; *American Scientist*

Goetz, David L.; *Death by Suburb*; 2006; Harper Collins

Haidt, Jonathan; *The Happiness Hypothesis*; 2006; Basic Books

Harford, Tim; *Adapt*; 2011; Farrar, Straus and Giroux

Harford, Tim; *The Logic of Life*; 2008; Random House

Heath, Chip & Heath, Dan; *Switch*; 2011; Broadway Books

Iyengar, Sheena; *The Art of Choosing*; 2011; Twelve Publishing

James, William; *The Principles of Psychology*; 1890, 1950; Dover Publications

Kahneman, Daniel; *Thinking, Fast and Slow*; 2011; Farrar, Straus and Giroux

Koch, Richard; *The 80/20 Principle*; 1998; Currency

Lupton, Robert D.; *Toxic Charity*; 2010; Harper One

Mauboussin, Michael J.; *More Than You Know*; 2008; Columbia University Press

McDougall, Christopher; *Born to Run*; 2009; Alfred A. Knopf

Moody, Harry R.; *The Five Stages of the Soul*; 1997; Anchor

Moore, Stephen & Simon, Julian L.; *It's Getting Better All the Time*; 2000; Cato Institute

Needleman, Jacob; *Money and the Meaning of Life*; 1991; Doubleday

Peters, Thomas J. & Waterman, Robert H.; *In Search of Excellence*; 1982; Warner Books

Pink, Daniel H.; *Drive*; 2009; Riverhead Books

Pink, Daniel H.; *A Whole New Mind*; 2006; Berkley Publishing Group

Ridley, Matt; *The Rational Optimist*; 2010; Harper Collins

Sadler, William A.; *The Third Age*; 2000; Da Capo Press

Schwartz, Barry; *The Paradox of Choice*; 2004; Harper Collins

Stanley, Thomas J.; *The Millionaire Mind*; 2001; Andrews McMeel Publishing

Stanley, Thomas J. & Danko, William D.; *The Millionaire Next Door*; 1996; Pocket Books

Thaler, Richard H. & Sunstein, Cass R.; *Nudge*; 2008; Yale University Press

Walker, Lewis; *Planning for the Challenges of Aging, Healthcare, and Special Needs*; 2012; FPA Press

Warren, Rick; *The Purpose Driven Life*; 2002; Zondervan

BECOMING WHEALTHY

WEB SITES

abcnews.go.com
authentichappiness.org
brainhealthhacks.com
calorieking.com
cnn.com
davidbeking.com
economist.com
edmunds.com
examiner.com
familydoctor.org
fivecentnickel.com
futurity.org
guardian.co.uk
heatherkampf.blogspot.com
huffingtonpost.com/natasha-dern
humanmetrics.com
illuminatedmind.net
livescience.com
livestrong.com
mayoclinic.com
medicinenet.com
myersbriggs.org
myfavouritemedicine.com
ncsu.edu/ffci/publications
onemedical.com
orlandosentinal.com
psychologytoday.com
psychosomaticmedicine.org
psych.rochester.edu/SDT
sciencedaily.com
sfchronicle.com
sidsavara.com

BECOMING WHEALTHY

sonoma.edu
statehealthfacts.org
stickK.com
time.com
topachievement.com
top10stop.com
usnews.com
usatoday.com
washingtonpost.com
wsj.com

www.ingramcontent.com/pod-product-compliance
Lightning Source LLC
Chambersburg PA
CBHW070602300426
44113CB00010B/1358